KEITH CHEETHAM's interest in Methodist heritage began during his schooldays in Sheffield, England. He attended the local Andover Street Methodist Church and in 1962 wrote and produced a pageant to celebrate the church's centenary.

In 1974 he was appointed as Sheffield's first Conference and Tourist Officer. Later elected as Chairman of the British Association of Conference Towns, he introduced the subject of John Wesley into various tourism promotions for his city (including in 1979 a commemorative re-enactment of Wesley's ride to Paradise Square, Sheffield, two hundred years earlier). In 1988 Keith was responsible, with the British Tourist Authority, for the research and introduction of a national tourist trail, *John Wesley's Britain*, which commemorated the 250th anniversary of the conversions of brothers John and Charles Wesley. In the same year he was invited to set up the Black Country Tourism Unit and become its Director. Some of his creative tourism schemes over the years won international recognition. Keith took early retirement in 1997 and now works as a freelance travel writer and tourism consultant.

He also continues as tourism advisor to the Heritage Committee of the Methodist Church and has been a key player, both locally and nationally, in the *John Wesley Tercentenary* celebrations in 2003. He has liaised extensively with the American Methodist Church and works with national tourist boards to attract more North American and other overseas visitors to Britain. Keith is also in heavy demand as a public speaker and a regular broadcaster on BBC Radio. Earlier books he has written include *Mary Queen of Scots – The Captive Years*, *On the Trail of Mary Queen of Scots*, and the best-selling *On the Trail of The Pilgrim Fathers*, of which the latter two are published by Luath Press.

Keith Cheetham also represents the Methodist Church on the Churches Tourism Association, which is aimed at attracting more visitors into churches and improving visitor facilities.

D1210572

15. 10. 09.

To Bob,

With every blessing !.

# On the Trail of
# John Wesley

*Keith*

KEITH CHEETHAM

*J. Keith Cheetham*

**Luath** Press Limited

EDINBURGH

www.luath.co.uk

First Published 2003

The paper used in this book is acid-free, neutral-sized and recyclable.
It is made from low chlorine pulps produced in a low energy,
low emission manner from renewable forests.

Printed and bound by
Bell & Bain Ltd., Glasgow

Typeset in Sabon 10.5 by Sarah Crozier, Nantes

# Acknowledgments

During the research, writing and compilation of this book, I have received an enormous amount of help, guidance and assistance from many people especially in connection with Methodist heritage. I have also received tremendous help from many Tourist Information Centres throughout Great Britain. I would especially like to mention John Lenton and the Rev. Donald Ryan M.Th, who have vetted my manuscript and without whose wise counselling and factual information this book could not have been completed. I should also like to mention the following people or bodies who have assisted me:

Noorah Al-Gailani, Wesley's Chapel, House, & Museum of Methodism, London; Sister Valerie Barker, Moravian Church, Chelsea; Rev. George Barton, Victoria Methodist Mission, Sheffield; Michael Bendall, Wesley's Chapel, London; Pamela Blakeman, Ely; Kenneth F Bowden, Bacup; David Brown, Kingswood School, Bath; Jo Coombs & Mrs EM Willy, South Petherton; Gillian Crawley, Gainsborough Old Hall; Irene Cunliffe, Mount Zion Chapel, Halifax; Dorset County Museum, Dorchester; Peter Forsaith & Rev Dr Tim McQuiban, Wesley & Methodist Studies Centre, Oxford Brookes University; Rev Philip Hoar & Mrs Joan Kilner, York; Helga Hughes, Red House Museum, Cleckheaton; Rev Terry Hurst, Brunswick Methodist Church, Newcastle-upon-Tyne; David T Heatherington, High House Chapel and Weardale Museum, Ireshopeburn, Co. Durham; Dawn Heywood, Dean Heritage Museum Trust; Rachel Juckes, Methodist Central Hall, Westminster; Randle Knight, William Salt Library, Stafford; Rev Paul King, Nicholson Square Methodist Church, Edinburgh; Rev Raymond King, Royal Tunbridge Wells; Mary Lowes, Newbiggin Methodist Chapel, Co. Durham; Martin Ludlow, Aldersgate Trust;

Barrie May, Cornish Museum of Methodism, Carharrack; Dave McGory, Coventry; Rev Dr Howard Mellor, Cliff College, Calver; Jim Merrington, Verwood, Dorset; Andrew Milson, Curator, Epworth Old Rectory; Dr Ken Mothersdale, Stourport; Marion Moverley, Richmond; David Nicoll, St John's Methodist Church, Arbroath; Ken Pooley, Wesley Cottage, Trewint; Rev Robin Roddie, Wesley Historical Society (Irish Branch); Rev Gethin Rhys, Coleg Trefeca, Brecon, Wales; Rev Barbara Savage, Matlock; Rev Derek Seber, Wirral; Gordon Simpson, Gordon Video Services; Rev Briant Smith, Isle of Wight; Professsor Charles Thomas, Gwithian Chapel, Cornwall; Mark Topping, John Wesley's Chapel, Bristol; Mark Turtle, photographer; Rev. Michael Walling, Canterbury; Fred Wharton, Christ Church, Oxford; Worcestershire History Centre; and John Young, Godalming Museum.

Finally, I should like to mention my colleague, David Middleton, for his line drawings; Jim Lewis, cartographer; Justin Crozier, editor; Tom Bee, designer; and my publishers at Luath Press, Audrey and Gavin MacDougall, who have, once again, given me every support and encouragement.

# Contents

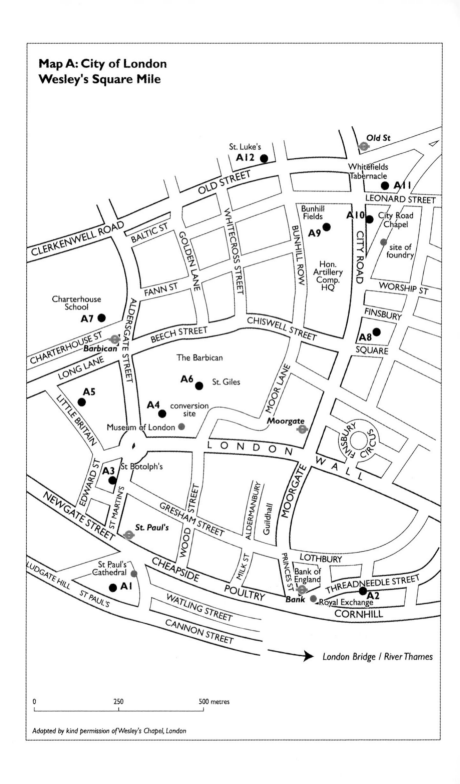

Map A: City of London
Wesley's Square Mile

St. Luke's
A12

Old St

Whitefields
Tabernacle
A11

LEONARD STREET

Bunhill
Fields
A9

A10

City Road
Chapel

site of
foundry

OLD STREET

BALTIC ST

CLERKENWELL ROAD

GOLDEN LANE

WHITECROSS STREET

BUNHILL ROW

CITY ROAD

WORSHIP ST

FANN ST

ALDERSGATE STREET

Hon.
Artillery
Comp.
HQ

FINSBURY

Charterhouse
School
A7

BEECH STREET

CHISWELL STREET

A8

CHARTERHOUSE ST

Barbican

SQUARE

LONG LANE

The Barbican

A6

St. Giles

MOOR LANE

LITTLE BRITAIN

A5

A4

conversion
site

Museum of London

Moorgate

L O N D O N        W A L L

FINSBURY CIRCUS

EDWARD ST

A3

St Botolph's

ST MARTIN'S

GRESHAM STREET

WOOD STREET

ALDERMANBURY

Guildhall

MOORGATE

NEWGATE STREET

St Paul's

CHEAPSIDE

MILK ST

PRINCES ST

LOTHBURY

Bank of
England

THREADNEEDLE STREET

LUDGATE HILL

St Paul's
Cathedral
A1

ST PAUL'S

POULTRY

Bank

Royal Exchange

A2

CORNHILL

WATLING STREET

CANNON STREET

London Bridge / River Thames

0        250        500 metres

Adapted by kind permission of Wesley's Chapel, London

## Key to Map A: City of London – Wesley's 'Square Mile'

**Ref**                                                                **Page(s)**

A1 – St Paul's Cathedral                    57, 58, 83, 84, 150, 205, 210
*John Wesley worshipped in Chancel prior to his conversion on 24 May 1738.*

A2 – Threadneedle Street                                          154
*Home of Mrs Molly Vazaille, the widow whom Wesley married in 1751.*

A3 – St Botolph's – Without-Aldersgate Parish Church, Aldersgate Street   43
*Rev Samuel Wesley Snr was curate for 12 months. Nearby at No. 12 Little Britain is plaque to mark site of Charles Wesley's conversion, 21 May 1738, three days prior to that of John.*

A4 – Conversion site and Museum of London                          82
*Near entrance to Museum of London in Nettleton Court is Methodist Flame commemorating John Wesley's conversion when his heart was 'strangely warmed' on 24 May 1738.*

A5 – St Bartholomew the Great Parish Church, West Smithfield        84
*Oldest London parish church. Wesley preached 6 times after debarment from other local churches.*

A6 – St Giles Parish Church, Cripplegate                          42, 84
*Rev Samuel Annesley, Susanna Wesley's father, was expelled for views on Uniformity.*

A7 – Charterhouse School, Charterhouse Street        35, 55, 58, 59, 60
*John Wesley a pupil between 1714-20. Once a Carthusian priory – traces still remain.*

A8 – Finsbury Square                                          94, 158
*Site in Moorfields area where George Whitefield, John and Charles Wesley preached.*

A9 – Bunhill Fields, off City Road                          157, 158
*Nonconformist burial ground with graves of Susanna Wesley (d. 1742), Isaac Watts, John Bunyan, Daniel Defoe, William Blake and other dissenters.*

A10 – Wesley's Chapel, Museum of Methodism        36, 161, 205, 209
and John Wesley's House, City Road
*Chapel built 1778 by John Wesley whose tomb is in graveyard at rear. See also Museum of Methodism. Adjacent is Wesley's house where he died on 2 March 1791 aged 87. Site of former Foundery to rear of Wesley's Chapel between Worship Street and Bonhill Street.*

A11 – Whitefield's Tabernacle, Leonard Street                      95
*Former site of wooden tabernacle built by Whitefield's followers. School now on site.*

A12 – St. Luke's Parish Church, Old Street                        84
*Only tower and shell remain of church, b.1732, once used by Foundery society, where Wesley and followers would have taken Communion in earlier years.*

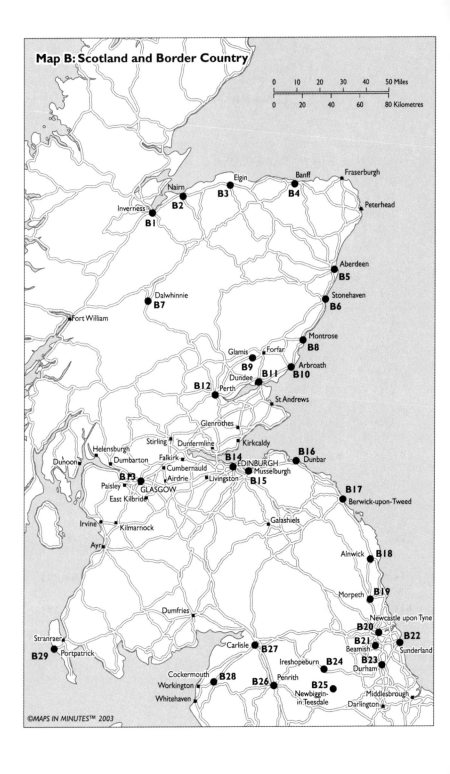

# Map B: Scotland and Border Country

0 10 20 30 40 50 Miles

0 20 40 60 80 Kilometres

Fraserburgh
Banff
**B4**
Peterhead
Elgin
**B3**
Nairn
**B2**
Inverness
**B1**

Aberdeen
**B5**
Stonehaven
**B6**
Dalwhinnie
**B7**
Fort William

Montrose
**B8**
Glamis
Forfar
**B9**
Dundee **B11**
Arbroath
**B10**
**B12** Perth
St Andrews
Glenrothes
Stirling
Dunfermline
Kirkcaldy
**B16** Dunbar
Helensburgh
**B14**
EDINBURGH
Dumbarton
Falkirk
Cumbernauld
Musselburgh
**B13**
Airdrie
Livingston
**B15**
Paisley
GLASGOW
East Kilbride
Dunoon
Irvine
Kilmarnock
Ayr
Galashiels

Berwick-upon-Tweed
**B17**

Alnwick **B18**

Morpeth **B19**

Dumfries
Newcastle upon Tyne
**B20**
Stranraer
**B21**
**B22**
Portpatrick
Beamish
Sunderland
**B29**
Carlisle
**B27**
**B23**
Durham
Ireshopeburn
**B24**
Cockermouth
**B28**
Penrith
Middlesbrough
Workington
**B26**
**B25**
Whitehaven
Newbiggin-
Darlington
in Teesdale

©MAPS IN MINUTES™ 2003

## Key to Map B: Scotland and Border Country

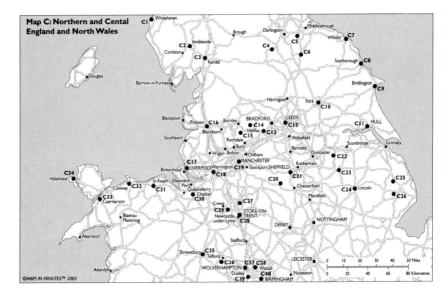

**Map C: Northern and Cental England and North Wales**

Whitehaven C1
Brough
Darlington
Middlesbrough
Whitby C7
Ambleside
C2 Coniston
C3 Kendal
C4
C5
C6
Scarborough C8
Barrow-in-Furness
Bridlington
C9
Harrogate
York
C10
Blackpool
Preston
C16 Burnley
BRADFORD
LEEDS
C12
HULL
C11
Blackburn
C15 Halifax
C14
C13
Wakefield
Scunthorpe
Grimsby
Southport
Rochdale
Bury
Barnsley
Doncaster
Wigan Bolton Oldham
MANCHESTER
Rotherham
C22
Birkenhead
C17 LIVERPOOL Warrington
C19 Stockport SHEFFIELD
C23
C25
Holyhead
C34
St Asaph Ellesmere
C18
C20
C21
C24 Lincoln
C26
Conway C32
Port
Chesterfield
Caernarvon
C33 C31
Queensferry
Chester
C30
Mansfield
Crewe
C29 C27
NOTTINGHAM
Blaenau Ffestiniog
Newcastle- C28
under-Lyme STOKE-ON-TRENT
DERBY
Abersoch
Stafford
Shrewsbury C35 Telford
LEICESTER
Aberdyfi
C36
C37 C38
WOLVERHAMPTON
Nuneaton
Dudley Walsall C40
C39 BIRMINGHAM

Douglas

0  10  20  30  40  50 Miles
0  20  40  60  80 Kilometres

©MAPS IN MINUTES™ 2003

## Key to Map C: Northern and Central England and North Wales

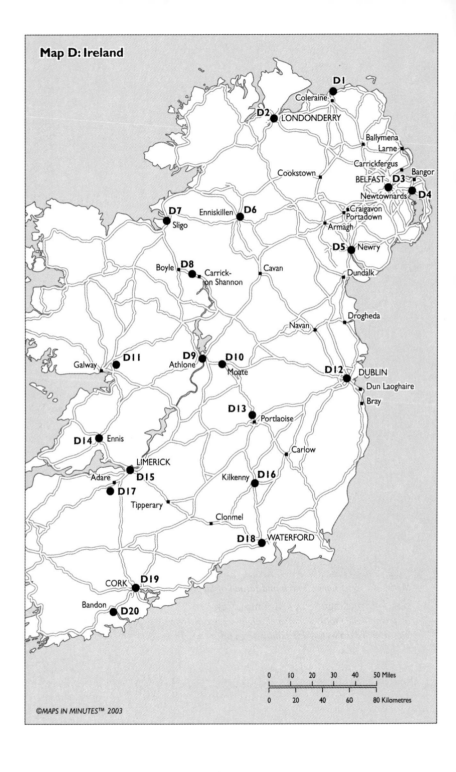

# Map D: Ireland

D1
Coleraine

D2
LONDONDERRY

Ballymena
Larne
Carrickfergus
Bangor
BELFAST D3
Newtownards D4

Cookstown

D7 Enniskillen D6
Sligo

Craigavon
Portadown
Armagh

D5 Newry
Dundalk

Boyle D8
Carrick-
on Shannon

Cavan

Drogheda

Navan

Galway D11

D9 D10
Athlone Moate

D12 DUBLIN
Dun Laoghaire
Bray

D13
Portlaoise

D14 Ennis

Carlow

LIMERICK
Adare D15
D17
Tipperary

Kilkenny D16

Clonmel

D18 WATERFORD

CORK D19
Bandon D20

0    10    20    30    40    50 Miles

0      20      40      60    80 Kilometres

©MAPS IN MINUTES™ 2003

## Map D: Ireland

| Ref. | Page(s) |
|---|---|

D1 – Coleraine and Giant's Causeway                                189, 190
*Wesley preached in Coleraine on four Irish tours and visited Giant's Causeway in 1778.*

D2 – Londonderry                                                              188
*Wesley paid 10 visits to Londonderry, holding meetings at the town hall and linen hall.*

D3 – Belfast and Lisburn                                             187, 188
*Wesley paid 12 visits to Belfast. Preached at market house, linen hall and St. Anne's Church. During 14 visits to Lisburn he often preached at linen hall. Nursed through illness in 1775.*

D4 – Newtownards                                                            188
*During 10 visits Wesley preached on Green, at Old Church and at Presbyterian church.*

D5 – Newry                                                                       187
*Wesley regularly preached in Newry. In 1767 delivered sermon Witness of the Spirit.*

D6 – Enniskillen                                                               190
*Wesley paid 6 visits. Preached in market house and Armstrong's house at nearby Sidaire.*

D7 – Sligo                                                                        188
*Visited on 13 tours, Wesley preached in old and new court houses, corn market and admired Dominican abbey. On last visit in 1789 he dined at the local military barracks.*

D8 – Boyle and Carrick-on-Shannon                                188
*In 1758 Wesley stated area was 'best populated part of Ireland he had seen so far'.*

D9 – Athlone                                                                     185
*On visit on 5 August 1752 Wesley preached 11 sermons in one day.*

D10 – Moate                                                                      185
*Described by Wesley on 1st visit in 1748 as 'pleasantest town... yet seen in Ireland.'*

D11 – Athenry                                                                   189
*Wesley made two visits to the town in 1785 and 1787.*

D12 – Dublin                                                          137, 183-189
*Wesley's main base in Ireland. Associated sites include St Patrick's Cathedral, Methodist Centenary Church and façade of Stephens Green Chapel.*

D13 – Portarlington and Mountmellick                             186
*In 1750 Wesley took 'first watch night service in Ireland' at Portarlington. Mountmellick also regular calling place to preach. In 1748, on 1st visit, Wesley preached whilst ill.*

D14 – Ennis and Clarecastle                                          187
*Wesley paid 6 visits to Ennis and 4 to Clarecastle and in 1773 stayed at local barracks.*

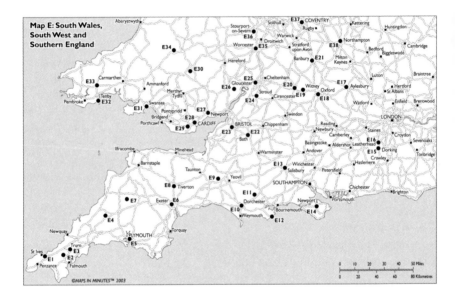

**Map E: South Wales, South West and Southern England**

Aberystwyth
Stourport-on-Severn
Solihull  **E37** COVENTRY  Rugby  Kettering  Huntingdon
Worcester  Warwick  Droitwich  **E38** Northampton  Bedford  Cambridge
**E36**  **E35**  Stratford upon Avon  Milton Keynes  Biggleswade
Hereford  Banbury  **E21**
**E34**
**E30**  Cheltenham  **E25**  **E20** Witney  Luton  Braintree
Carmarthen  **E26** Gloucester  Oxford  **E17** Aylesbury  Hertford  St Albans
**E33**  Ammanford  Merthyr Tydfil  Stroud  **E19**  **E18**  Watford  Enfield  Brentwood
Tenby  **E32**  Pontypridd  **E24** Cirencester  LONDON
Pembroke  **E31** Swansea  **E27** Newport  Swindon  Reading
Porthcawl  **E28**  BRISTOL  Chippenham  Newbury  Camberley  Staines  Croydon
Bridgend  **E29**  CARDIFF  **E23**  **E22**  Basingstoke  Aldershot  Leatherhead  **E16** Sevenoaks
Ilfracombe  Minehead  Bath  Warminster  Andover  Haslemere  Dorking  **E15** Crawley  Tonbridge
Barnstaple  Taunton  **E13** Winchester  Petersfield
**E8**  **E9** Yeovil  Salisbury  SOUTHAMPTON  Chichester  Brighton
Newquay  **E7**  Tiverton  **E11**  Portsmouth
**E4**  Exeter  **E6**  Dorchester  Newport  **E14**
St Ives  Truro  Torquay  **E10** Weymouth  Bournemouth  **E12**
**E1**  **E3**  PLYMOUTH  **E5**
Penzance  **E2** Falmouth

0   10   20   30   40   50 Miles
0   20   40   60   80 Kilometres

©MAPS IN MINUTES™ 2003

## Map E: South Wales, South West and Southern England

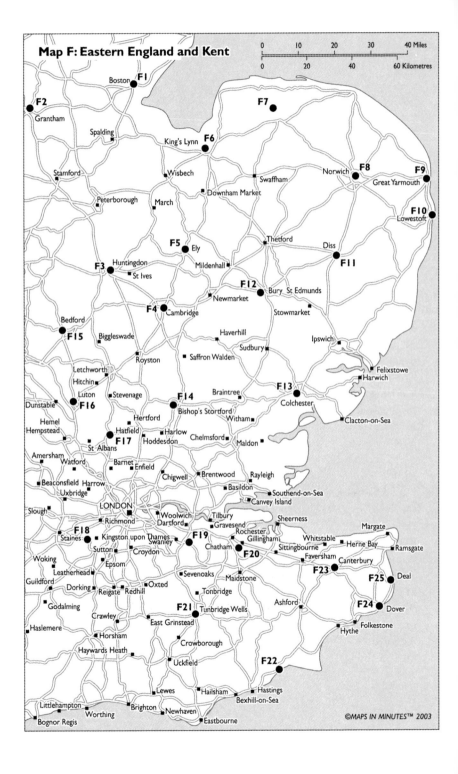

# Map F: Eastern England and Kent

0    10    20    30    40 Miles
0    20    40    60 Kilometres

Boston **F1**
**F2**
Grantham
Spalding
**F7**
Stamford
King's Lynn **F6**
Wisbech
Norwich **F8**
**F9**
Great Yarmouth
Peterborough
March
Downham Market
Swaffham
**F10**
Lowestoft
**F5** Ely
Thetford
Diss
Huntingdon
Mildenhall
**F11**
**F3**
St Ives
**F12**
Bury St Edmunds
Newmarket
Bedford
**F4** Cambridge
Stowmarket
Biggleswade
Haverhill
Ipswich
**F15**
Sudbury
Royston
Felixstowe
Letchworth
Saffron Walden
Harwich
Hitchin
Braintree
**F13**
Luton
Stevenage
**F14**
Colchester
Dunstable **F16**
Bishop's Stortford
Clacton-on-Sea
Hemel
Hertford
Witham
Hempstead
Hatfield
Harlow
Chelmsford
Amersham
St Albans **F17**
Hoddesdon
Maldon
Watford
Barnet
Enfield
Beaconsfield
Harrow
Chigwell
Brentwood
Rayleigh
Uxbridge
Basildon
Southend-on-Sea
Slough
LONDON
Canvey Island
Sheerness
Richmond
Woolwich
Tilbury
Margate
**F18**
Dartford
Gravesend
Staines
Kingston upon Thames **F19**
Rochester
Whitstable
Herne Bay
Ramsgate
Sutton
Swanley
Chatham
Gillingham
Sittingbourne
Woking
Epsom
Croydon
**F20**
Faversham
Canterbury
**F23**
Leatherhead
Sevenoaks
Maidstone
**F25** Deal
Guildford
Dorking
Oxted
Reigate Redhill
Tonbridge
Ashford
**F24** Dover
Godalming
Crawley
**F21** Tunbridge Wells
Hythe
Folkestone
Haslemere
East Grinstead
Horsham
Crowborough
Haywards Heath
Uckfield
**F22**
Lewes
Hailsham
Hastings
Littlehampton
Brighton
Newhaven
Bexhill-on-Sea
Bognor Regis
Worthing
Eastbourne

©MAPS IN MINUTES™ 2003

## Map F: Eastern England and Kent

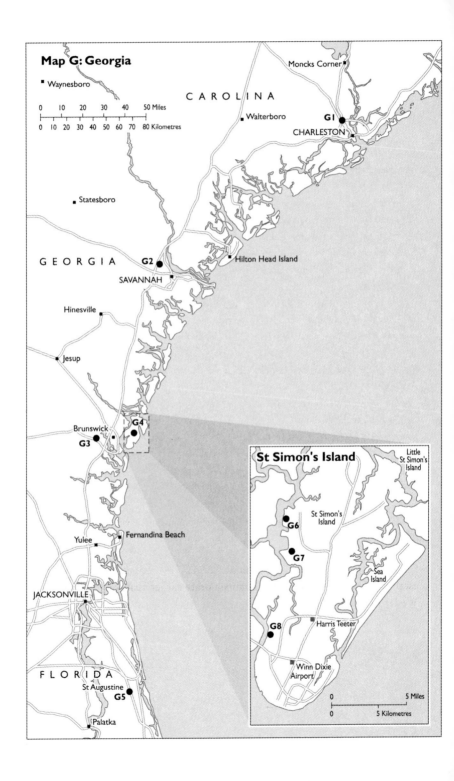

## Map G: Georgia

- Waynesboro

0  10  20  30  40  50 Miles
0 10 20 30 40 50 60 70 80 Kilometres

CAROLINA

Moncks Corner ■

Walterboro ■

**G1** ●
CHARLESTON ■

- Statesboro

GEORGIA

**G2** ●
SAVANNAH ■

■ Hilton Head Island

Hinesville ■

Jesup ●

**G4** ●
Brunswick ●
**G3** ●

Yulee ●        ■ Fernandina Beach

JACKSONVILLE ●

FLORIDA

St Augustine ■
**G5** ●

Palatka ●

### St Simon's Island

Little
St Simon's
Island

St Simon's
Island

**G6** ●

**G7** ●

Sea
Island

**G8** ●        ■ Harris Teeter

■ Winn Dixie
Airport

0                5 Miles
0                5 Kilometres

## Map G: Georgia

# Foreword

MY FIRST INTEREST in John Wesley started as a fourteen-year old schoolboy in my native city of Sheffield. Having a reasonable boy soprano voice, I was invited to become a chorister at Sheffield's Anglican Cathedral although I had been brought up a Methodist. My music master at Nether Edge Grammar School, Mr CHC Biltcliffe, advised me to join a good church choir as part of my voice training and the experience proved invaluable in years to come.

In 1951 the Methodist Conference was held in Sheffield (an annual gathering to discuss matters of policy, spirituality and other church-related subjects). During that period, members of the Cathedral choir processed the short distance into Paradise Square, a lovely cobble-stoned Georgian square on the northern side of the cathedral precincts. It has many buildings of character, both from Georgian and Victorian periods. For many years the square had been a meeting place of townsfolk for political, religious and other gatherings, whether it be to demonstrate, riot or even worship. From its earliest history it was the site of a market. The square's sloping surface and raised balcony at No.18, once a Freemasons' Lodge, made it an ideal place for outdoor meetings.

One of the most influential people ever to address the people of Sheffield from that balcony, then reached by a flight of steps to the original first floor doorway, was John Wesley. He first visited the town in 1742 when a Methodist society was worshipping at a house in Cheyney Square, later destroyed by a mob of rioters. On 15 July 1779, Wesley came to Sheffield to address a meeting in Paradise Square and people flocked to hear him. Afterwards, John Wesley wrote in his journal that he 'preached to the largest congregation he ever saw on a weekday'.

It was at a commemoration of this event that I went along with the Cathedral choir to sing at the unveiling of a plaque on the south side of the square. One person present at the ceremony was prominent Methodist and famous film magnate, Mr J Arthur

Rank (later Lord Rank). At the time a suggestion was made that perhaps one day he might consider making a film about John Wesley's life. A couple of years or so later, the great man did just that. The actor who played the role of Wesley was Leonard Sachs, perhaps better known as Chairman in the BBC's long running series *The Good Olde Days* which was regularly televised from the City Varieties Theatre in Leeds, West Yorkshire.

Some years later, in 1979 as Sheffield's first Conference and Tourism Officer, I helped organise a re-enactment of the 1779 event – exactly two hundred years to the day of Wesley preaching in Paradise Square. By then I was a member of the Methodist Church and involved in Methodist heritage. This intensified in 1988 when I was co-opted by the British Tourist Authority to help research and produce a *John Wesley's Britain* trail leaflet. It was produced to commemorate the 250th anniversary of the conversions of both John Wesley and his younger brother, Charles, which took place within a day or two of eachother. On that occasion at a meeting in Aldersgate Street, London, John Wesley wrote 'he had felt his heart strangely warmed'.

Over the years my work and research has covered wider areas of Methodism – especially the early growth of the American Methodist Church, much enhanced by the work of West Bromwich-born Francis Asbury, one of John Wesley's itinerant preachers who volunteered to 'spread the Gospel' across the Atlantic in the New World. He was ordained as its first Bishop in 1784. As tourism advisor to the Heritage Committee of the Methodist Church and member of the National Churches Tourism Association, I am even more involved with Christian heritage, embracing other denominations and related sites both of an historical and contemporary nature. The year 2003 is the tercentenary of the birth of John Wesley and countrywide celebrations are planned. These will not only commemorate his life but also demonstrate and celebrate how his teachings still relate to the lives of Christians in the modern world. There is still much to learn from the lessons and examples of the past.

*J Keith Cheetham*

# Introduction

JOHN WESLEY WAS the founder of Methodism which has spread to almost every country in the world and has a membership of some seventy million people. The name Methodist was first attributed to Wesley and his fellow students who formed the 'Holy Club' when they were at university in Oxford. It was a nickname given to the group by fellow students who, mockingly, made fun of the methodical approach its members adopted from the Bible for developing personal devotion and putting its teachings into practice. Though ordained as a priest in the Church of England, Wesley's later decision to employ lay preachers and preach outdoor sermons angered Church authorities and he was accused of being a Nonconformist. (A Nonconformist or Dissenter was one who refused to abide by the doctrines and policy of the established Church of England. In England and Wales, the Nonconformist Churches are Protestant. They include Methodists, Baptists, Congregationalists (now United Reformed), Friends (Quakers), and the Brethren. In Scotland, where the established Church is Presbyterian, the Scottish Episcopal Church is Nonconformist. They differed from the Anglican Church over matters of doctrine, worship and church government.) Despite John Wesley's high-church views, his influence seemed to possess something of a Puritan spirit, first experienced in the previous century. His own spiritual journey was turbulent with regular displays of recklessness and self-will.

In over fifty years of evangelising Wesley preached at least 40,000 sermons (often several in a day) and travelled 250,000 miles (402,325 km) – mainly on horseback but in later years by carriage. He and his brother Charles were at the forefront of the great evangelical Revival of the 18th century brought about by a wave of religious enthusiasm and fervour emulated by powerful preachers such as the two Wesley brothers, George Whitefield, and some of their contemporaries. Hundreds of books have been written about John Wesley and his impact on international religious history. It started with Wesley's own Journals (diaries) which, for most of his adult life, give a day-by-day account of his travels and activities throughout many parts of Britain, Ireland, Germany and places in America. To attempt to trace his life and events in chronological order in such a publication as this would be impossible. I therefore aim to explore different aspects of his character, covering important events and describing, as appropriate, places, backgrounds and the periods of history in which they appear. There are many historic sites connected with early Methodism and my intention is to highlight their relevance to the story.

The vast majority of books about the Wesleys (I use this term in the context of the whole family rather than John alone) tend to be written on subjects of spirituality, family history, church music, social and political aspects, or Wesleyan sermons. Few have actually dealt with early Methodism from the traveller or tourist's point of view. Exceptions over recent years have included the informative *In The Steps Of John Wesley* by Frederick C Gill (1962); an excellent series of booklets published by Methodist Publishing House for the World Methodist Historical Society (British Section) – *A Methodist Guide To London and the South-East* by John Vickers & Betty Young (1980), – *Lincolnshire and East Anglia* by William Leary and John Vickers (1984) – *Cornwall* by Thomas Shaw (1991), – *Bristol and the South-West* by John Edwards, Peter Gentry and Roger Thorne (1991); and finally *Exploring Scotland With Wesley* published by The Synod of The Methodist Church in Scotland (1989).

*On the Trail of John Wesley* sets out to describe, fairly simply, many sites connected with Wesley and his followers which, in the main, are tabulated in a separate section of maps of geographical areas covering his travels. Specific locations are cross-referenced to the main text of the book. He preached his sermons – mostly extempore and in the open air – in cities, towns, villages and the open countryside, in fact, in thousands of places – so there is no way that every place at which he preached can be covered in one book. I therefore apologise, in advance, if any particular Wesleyan place or site known to a reader is not included.

Wesley was not the best of all preachers in Methodism – this accolade was attributed to George Whitefield, a more charismatic orator, who first introduced John to preaching in the open air – a practice which infringed both civil and ecclesiastical laws. However, in preaching, it was Wesley who delivered the more invoking sermons. His message was simple – that Jesus Christ died for all sinners. 'Salvation by Faith' through Jesus was the main theme and he toiled endlessly to the end of his days to pass on this inspired utterance to others. Whitefield was a Calvinist (one who followed the doctrines of John Calvin, a Genevan Protestant reformer, who laid special emphasis on the sovereignty of God in the conferring of grace). Calvinists considered that only those chosen by God would be saved. On the other hand, Wesley's message was for all.

Whilst the emphasis of the book is on John and his fellow preachers, let us not forget the enormous contribution towards the growth of Methodism made by his younger brother Charles, who wrote over seven thousand hymns, many of which have remained well-known up to present day. He and his musical family played an important role in helping the world 'sing the praises' of Christianity. On the other hand, the work of both brothers meant that they were also champions of the Christian faith which kept Britain, almost singly in Europe, from stormy revolutionary politics. Their story is a remarkable one.

John Wesley's own life was complex yet dedicated in his pursuit of spreading the Word of God amongst fellow human beings along the 'highways and byways' where he travelled. He disregarded parochial and diocesan boundaries, going where he felt God was calling him. The popular image which developed over the years is of an ethereal figure without blemish. He was, however, a human being with feelings like the rest of us and also had many faults. On Church matters John usually turned to his father, Samuel, but since childhood had worshipped his mother, Susanna. It was to her whom he turned on all spiritual and moral issues. In his relationships with the opposite sex he seemed to be seeking a prototype of his mother. These liaisons were not always successful and John found it difficult to form a satisfactory relationship, as in his unfortunate marriage with Mrs Vazeille.

He inspired and influenced thousands of people during his lifetime leaving a legacy of worldwide proportions. He always remained an Anglican priest even though the Methodist Church developed from his brilliant organisation of the class and circuit system, the building of many chapels, and his preaching to a largely non-Establishment society in Britain. John lived during the early period of the Industrial Revolution when many from a largely rural population flocked to new industrial towns to find employment. Times were changing and Wesley, from the point of his conversion, pursued with vigour and great enthusiasm his calling to preach the Gospel to the 'unconverted'.

I trust that if you have not already been so, you also might be inspired by John Wesley and his teachings. If you are led by this book to a deeper commitment in your own life to Jesus Christ or indeed just wish to follow 'the trail of John Wesley', then my efforts will have been amply rewarded.

*J Keith Cheetham*
April 2003

# Chronology of John Wesley
# and Early Methodism

| | |
|---|---|
| 1703 | 17 June: John Wesley born, Epworth, Lincolnshire. |
| 1707 | 18 December: Charles Wesley born, Epworth, Lincolnshire. |
| 1709 | Fire at Epworth Rectory – John Wesley rescued. |
| 1714 | Admitted to Charterhouse School, London. |
| 1720 | Undergraduate at Christ Church, Oxford. |
| 1725 | Ordained deacon in Christ Church Cathedral. |
| 1726 | Elected Fellow of Lincoln College, Oxford. |
| 1728 | 22 September: Ordained Anglican priest in Christ Church Cathedral. |
| 1730 | Becomes leader of 'The Holy Club' at Oxford. |
| 1735 | 25 April: Death of Samuel Wesley Snr, Epworth, aged 72; 14 October: John and Charles Wesley depart for Georgia. |
| 1736 | 3 December: Charles Wesley returns from Georgia. |
| 1738 | 1 February: John Wesley returns from Georgia 'unfulfilled'; 24 May: 'Aldersgate experience', 'I felt my heart strangely warmed.' |

1739     17 February: George Whitefield starts open air preaching at Kingswood; 8 April: John Wesley follows his example at Hanham Mount; May: Work begins on building of Bristol's 'New Room' chapel; December: Methodist Society meets Old Foundery, Moorfields, London.
English-speaking Welsh Wesleyan Methodism starts.

1740     Wesley severs connection with Moravians. He employs lay preachers and build chapels. Wesley and Whitefield agree to differ over doctrine of predestination.

1742     23 July: Death of Susanna Wesley, London, aged 73

1743     Methodists produce rules for 'classes'
Welsh Calvinistic Methodist Church founded from revival activities of Howell Harris and Daniel Rowland; Anti-Methodist rioting in Wednesbury and the Black Country

1744     First Methodist Conference at Foundery Chapel, London

1747     John Wesley's first visits Ireland.
Methodist societies group into circuits

1749     Calvinists under Whitefield desert Wesley.
Whitefield becomes chaplain to Lady Huntingdon.

1751     John Wesley's marries Mrs Molly Vazeille (they separate 1755).

1771     4 September: Francis Asbury sails for America as Wesleyan missionary.

1778   1 November: Wesley's Chapel opens, City Road, London.

1781   Lady Huntingdon's Calvinist Church separates from Church of England.

1784   Wesley signs Deed of Declaration – giving legal status to Methodist preachers after his death; Dr Thomas Coke ordained by Wesley as 'superintendent' of Methodist society in America. Coke ordains Francis Asbury as first Bishop; Methodist Episcopal Church of America established.

1788   20 March: Death of Charles Wesley, London, aged 80.

1791   2 March: Death of John Wesley at house in City Road, London, aged 87.
9 March: Buried in vault at graveyard of Wesley's Chapel, City Road, London.

1795   Plan of Pacification accepted by Wesleyan Conference leads to separation of Methodists from Church of England.

1797   Methodist New Connexion inaugurated.

1800   Welsh-speaking Wesleyan Methodism starts.

1807 –  Primitive Methodist Connexion formed by Hugh
1812   Bourne and William Clowes, Staffordshire.

1815   Formation of Bible Christians by William O'Bryan, Cornwall.

From the 1730s until his death, John Wesley travelled many

thousands of miles around Britain and Ireland – on horseback or by carriage – preaching several times each day (a total of 40,000 sermons), and writing or editing some 400 publications. He left behind a movement of about 70,000 members.

# CHAPTER I

# A Marriage Made In Heaven?

SAMUEL WESLEY IS CONSIDERED to be 'the father of the Wesley family'. He is known to have descended from a distinguished pedigree and could trace his ancestors back to the period before the Norman conquest. One had been in the Holy Land at the time of the Crusades. Another was Adam Loftus (1553-1605), primate of Ireland but his more immediate family, on both sides, was Nonconformist. Samuel was the son and grandson of Church of England, later Nonconformist, clergy and was to become the father of John and Charles Wesley, the two most famous of his children.

Samuel was born in the sleepy village of Winterborne Whitechurch (E11) in Dorset in November 1662 where his father, John, was vicar (the 15th century font in which Samuel was baptized can be seen in the tiny St. Mary's Church). His father died when he was quite young so Samuel was brought up by his widowed mother who soon set about making sure the boy was given a good formal education. She must have realised that at an early age her son was beginning to show much promise and so found him a place at the Free School in Dorchester (E10) under Mr Henry Dolling. The school, founded in 1569 and situated in South Street, burnt down in 1613. It was rebuilt five years later but demolished in 1832. The area around Dorchester was known as being very Protestant with strong leanings towards Nonconformity.

During the reigns of Queen Elizabeth I and her successor, James I of England and VI of Scotland, many changes had begun to take place in the Established Church as set up by Henry VIII in 1534. Despite the break from the Roman Catholic Church and the establishment of the Church of England (Anglican Church), a growing number of Protestants felt these changes had not gone far enough. This was the start of the Puritan movement – people who wished to 'purify' the Church – and gradually groups of Dissenters began to appear. In the main, these were from rural parishes and the Bishops and higher echelons of the clergy did what they could to suppress these outbreaks. Any clergyman found not to be conforming to Anglican doctrines was routed out, persecuted and stripped of his living. However some Nonconformists decided that enough was enough and sought religious freedom in Holland and other Low Countries of Europe; others sailed across the Atlantic to the New World where new colonies had opened up to emigrants. Those Dissenters, better known as the Pilgrim Fathers, are perhaps the most celebrated among them, having left Plymouth (E5), Devon, in September 1620 on an historic journey on the Mayflower bound for a new life in the New World.

Much of the unrest had come about from the translation of the Bible into the English language during the 16th century. This opened up new and wider possibilities for people who could read but were not educated in foreign languages such as Latin – the language of the medieval Church. It meant that any reader could now study the Bible. Consequently, groups of people started to meet together to read, worship and discuss their thoughts and findings as well as listen to the words of preachers. From these small beginnings, the tradition of family prayers was established, more in keeping with the simplicity of New Testament tradition.

In particular, groups of academics and students at both Oxford (E18) and Cambridge (F4) universities (at which only members of the Church of England were allowed to study) began to examine the teachings of the Bible for themselves. Thus began a wave of enthusiasm for Nonconformity and a growing indoctrination of would-be Anglican clergymen. Such meetings had to be conducted clandestinely as law decreed that no Nonconformist be permitted to attend either university.

Samuel Wesley's own father, John, and grandfather, Bartholomew, were just two students who were influenced by such teachers whilst at university. It is therefore no surprise that the young Samuel would have been told tales of his immediate family and the hardships they had had to endure because of their leanings towards Nonconformity. It was to play an important role in his own background as he grew to manhood. Bartholomew Wesley was ejected from his living as Rector at Charmouth near Lyme Regis in Dorset in 1662 by the Act of Uniformity. This act, imposed after the restoration of Charles II, required that all clergy of the Church of England accept without question 'all and everything contained and prescribed' in the revised Book of Common Prayer, making it the standard of belief and worship. Bartholomew's son, John (Samuel's father), was also deprived of his post at the church in Winterbourne Whitechurch after being committed to prison for his refusal to use the Book of Common Prayer. Two thousand other priests in the Church of England had also left their incumbencies at the same time because they refused to accept the principles of the Act.

Young Samuel's own leanings towards Nonconformity encouraged others to offer him assistance to help train him for the ministry. By that time, Oxford and Cambridge university authorities had clamped down on students whom they termed as Nonconformists entering their portals. Those who wished to study the new approach had to seek alternative training elsewhere. The answer was that Dissenting Academies were established to offer a similar education as that given by the established seats of learning.

Consequently, from Dorchester Free School Samuel was sent to an academy in the Stepney area of London run by a Dr Veale. Later, he attended a similar establishment, Newington Green in nearby Stoke Newington, under Mr Charles Morton. This was another private school for Nonconformists to help prepare them to become members of the clergy in that movement. At this establishment he was to meet fellow student Daniel Defoe, who was later to write the novels *Robinson Crusoe* and *Moll Flanders*. Whilst at Morton's academy Samuel undertook a rigorous study of Nonconformity and came to the conclusion that it was not for him despite his father's and grandfather's own beliefs. Neither would it lead to his making a living in the Church of England. It was also during his stay in London that he first met Susanna Annesley, possibly at her parents' home at Spital Yard, a cul-de-sac between Spital Square and Bishopsgate Street, close to the present Liverpool Street railway station (the house is marked by a wall plaque). She was born at the three-storeyed establishment on 20 January 1669. Her parents were Dr Samuel Annesley, former Vicar of St Giles, Cripplegate (A6), one of the largest churches in London (from which he also had been ejected in 1662 for Nonconformity) and his second wife, surnamed White. (Dr Annesley was born near Kenilworth in 1620, received a primary education at the Coventry free grammar school (E37), and later went up to university at Oxford.) Susanna was noted for her good looks and was her father's twenty-fifth child and her mother's twenty-fourth. Dr Annesley later became the minister of the Puritan meetinghouse in St Helen's Place. He is said to have been in the habit of reading twenty chapters of the Bible every day in the attic of their house.

Susanna, along with her brothers and sisters, was educated at home and, by the time she was thirteen, had formed her own opinions on Nonconformity and the Church of England. She disagreed with her father's stance on the matter and, determinedly, took steps to return to the Anglican Church. Her father's opinion on the matter is not recorded but he must have realised that the young girl had spirit and was strong-minded.

Samuel Wesley was aware that most ordained priests had had to learn their profession by way of Oxford or Cambridge University and felt he should follow the same course. He therefore set off from London on foot in 1683 to try and secure a place at Oxford. With little money to pay for his training at Exeter College he managed to obtain a job as a servitor. This meant he became a male attendant, an undergraduate partly supported by college funds, whose role was to wait on the 'fellows and gentlemen commoners' at the table and assist with other duties. By these means Samuel was able to continue with his studies.

Throughout his time at the University he kept in touch with Susanna by writing letters. After four years he graduated with a Bachelor of Arts degree in June 1688 and decided his way forward was to apply for ordination as a priest in the Church of England. On achieving this in February 1689, it was natural that he should gravitate towards London to seek a post that would allow him to be nearer to Susanna.

They soon discovered that, despite their respective upbringings, their opinions on the subject of Nonconformity were mutual. In addition, they each had literary and theological gifts and shared many similarities. These attributes would have automatically drawn them closer together along with the fact that they came from similar family backgrounds. Although very different in temperament, they were both people of standing and intellect – and soon fell in love.

Samuel was eventually offered a post of curate at St Botolph-Without-Aldersgate Church (A3), situated on Aldersgate Street at the corner with Little Britain (so called because the surrounding area was actually bequeathed to the Count of Brittany after the Norman Conquest and became known as Little Brittany. The name has been shortened over the years.).

St Botolph's church has a modest late Georgian exterior, completed in 1791. The interior has a finely-decorated plaster ceiling, a rich brown wooden organ case and original pews retained in the galleries. The church also has a late 18th century stained glass window of John Wesley preaching near to the Foundery in London and a commemorative plaque relating to the Wesley connection is attached to the railings of the churchyard. At the rear of the building is a shelter containing plaques dedicated to children of the city of London who died in heroic circumstances.

Samuel married Susanna on 12 November 1688 at the former St Marylebone Parish Church on Marylebone Road whilst still a curate of St Botolph's. (Lord Byron was later christened at the same church in 1778 but it was rebuilt and re-consecrated in 1817. Poets Robert Browning and Elizabeth Barrett were married in the new building in 1846).

At their own marriage Samuel Wesley was 27 and Susanna nearly 20. They had barely been married a year before Samuel, after much soul-searching, decided to take up a post as ship's chaplain in an effort to bring in more income than his meagre salary of thirty pounds as a curate. The parting was only temporary but during that time Susanna returned to live with her parents where she gave birth to her first child, Samuel Jnr, in February 1690.

On his return to shore, Samuel saw his four-month-old child for the first time and decided that a life at sea was no longer acceptable. He managed to obtain a curacy in Surrey on a temporary basis until a better offer came his way. This arrived in the form of a living at South Ormsby (C25) in the county of Lincolnshire, offered to him by the patron of the living, John Sheffield, 1st Duke of Buckingham and Normanby, a local landowner who made Samuel his chaplain. South Ormsby is set in a quiet wooded area on the rolling Lincolnshire Wolds and its church is situated at the highest point of the village. It has a fine Western Tower with large gargoyles and crocketed pinnacles and contains five bells originally hung in 1757. The Rectory where Samuel and his family lived was a lath and wattle building in parkland below the church. It was demolished in 1850 and a new building was erected on an alternative site. The present Hall in the park was rebuilt in 1752-55 by James Paine and contains a fine Georgian staircase carved by William Lumby. There are many picturesque cottages dotted about the village.

Samuel and Susanna's family soon began to expand with six more children born while they lived at South Ormsby. Three died in infancy and were buried in the churchyard. In general, life was quite pleasant until the mistress of John Sanderson (later to become Lord Castleton), the local squire, struck up a friendship with Susanna and started to visit the Rectory. Samuel was displeased and ordered the woman away!

In 1695 an opportunity arose for Samuel to gain promotion within the Church of England when he was offered the post of Rector at the parish church of St Andrew's in the small town of

Epworth (C22) in the same county. In no way could he have realised just what great changes or indeed controversies in the Established Church this move would lead to. It was initially to transform the religious face of Britain and would later have worldwide implications.

# CHAPTER 2

# Early Days at Epworth

THE ISLE OF AXHOLME is so named because it is a piece of land bounded by four rivers – the Don to the north, the Torne in the west, the Idle to the south, and the Trent in the east. At the centre of this rural community stands the little town of Epworth in an area now designated as North Lincolnshire.

In the time of the Britons and Romans the Isle of Axholme formed the northern territory of the Coritani, the ancient inhabitants of the county of Lincoln. Britons from the forest areas to the east frequently tried to harass the Romans travelling from Lindum (Lincoln) to Danum (Doncaster) where they kept a standing garrison. Eventually a battle was fought and won around AD 50 by the Romans, who, in reprisal, set fire to the forest.

In Saxon times, the Isle became part of the northern boundary of the kingdom of Mercia not far from its boundary with the kingdom of Northumbria. Consequently, cross-border squabbles were commonplace. In AD 632 Penda, the pagan ruler of Mercia, confronted Edwin of Northumbria at nearby Hatfield where a battle took place. Edwin was routed and slain in the action. Nine years later Penda also slew in battle the pious King Oswald of Northumbria. Later, the parish church at nearby Crowle was dedicated to St Oswald. In AD 829 Northumbria was brought under the overlordship of Ecgbert of Wessex, who also claimed dominion over Mercia, when he met Eanred of Northumbria at a place called Dore, a pretty south-western suburb of the city of Sheffield (C21).

It is thought the reference to St Oswald in the Isle of Axholme is the first intimation of a Christian church in the area. By the time of William the Conqueror, the Bishop of Coutances in

France had been granted estates in the northern part of Lincolnshire which were passed to his nephew Robert de Mowbray. He was to fall from grace on his opposition to William Rufus and died a captive at Windsor in 1106. In the reign of Henry I the manor of Epworth and Westwoodside was conferred on Nigel d'Albini, a renowned soldier close to William Rufus. His son, Roger, assumed by royal mandate the arms and name of de Mowbray, a family name which has long been associated with Epworth and surrounding estates. Down the years various members of the family held prominent and distinguished positions. For instance, in 1215 William de Mowbray was the most resolute of the 25 barons who compelled King John to sign the Magna Carta. Another member of the family, John de Mowbray, in 1326, gave his tenants free use of all the waste lands around Epworth. Thomas de Mowbray, in 1385, was made Earl Marshal of England and later became Duke of Norfolk. Vinegarth, the family mansion, once stood next to St Andrew's Parish Church but is now demolished. Excavations on the site during the 1970s revealed marlstone foundations and a tiled floor bearing the family's coat of arms.

St Andrew's Parish Church is approached from the medieval market cross at the centre of the small town of Epworth along a broad stone-flagged avenue of lime trees. It stands on raised ground and dominates the surrounding area. On passing through the gate one approaches the imposing south porch (to the right is a pathway which leads to the restored tomb of the Reverend Samuel Wesley). The centre portion of the church dates back to the 12th century but the building in its present form includes features from other periods. The Chancel arch and aisle arcades are Early English. A two-light window in the West End of the North Aisle and other windows are from the Decorated period as is the North Porch. The church tower belongs to the Perpendicular style of architecture and, when built, the inside buttresses encroached on the arcading. It contains a fine peal of eight bells, the largest weighing 869 kilograms with a diameter of 1 metre 22 centimetres. In 1642, the church was ransacked by fanatics when the Civil War broke out and the structure fell into decay. Some parts had to be demolished and the building stayed in a sad state of disrepair for some years.

As one enters the church today, one's eyes are drawn to an old 16th century parish chest and the church font. The latter would certainly have been in use when the Wesley children were baptized by Samuel, their father. Standing within the Sanctuary are a fine altar and two 16th century wooden chairs. One is thought to have been given by Susanna before she left Epworth. The other has an inscription of 1560 on the back. The church authorities also own a silver chalice which was the one used by John Wesley when he took his first communion at the age of eight.

The northern parts of Lincolnshire and Nottinghamshire had been a hotbed of Nonconformity for some years. In the early part of the 17th century, the Separatist movement had started in nearby Gainsborough under John Smyth, and a similar group originated in the villages of Babworth and Scrooby, both within a 15-mile (24 km) radius of Epworth. Most of these folk had fled to Holland or on to the New World as part of the original contingent of Pilgrim Fathers. In 1660, over thirty Quakers in the area were imprisoned for attending religious meetings. The Baptist movement was also well established in the area since 1673. It meant that the Islonians (the name given to local people) had become a parochial yet fiercely independent folk, especially in their opposition to the Established Church. There would be antagonism towards whoever was imposed upon them as rector.

The wind-swept Isle of Axholme and adjacent areas are very flat and for many years the once-wooded lands destroyed by the Romans were water-logged. Charles I allowed Dutch engineers to drain the marshes under the direction of Cornelius Vermuyden. The idea was to open up more land for agricultural purposes. The construction of dikes helped drain the land (There is also much evidence of Flemish architecture in numerous buildings which were erected in the Isle of Axholme at that time – the post office in Epworth is a prime example). The arrangement was that

Vermuyden was to be given one third of any new land which might be reclaimed and this angered local people. It meant they were about to lose their rights to use the waste lands first granted to them in 1326. As a result the King and the Established Church fell out of favour with the parishioners and the place soon became a centre of both political and religious unrest. This was the scenario which faced the new rector.

Samuel, Susanna and their family of four children arrived at Epworth in 1696 to live at the rectory. (The site of the original rectory destroyed by fire in 1709 was the same as the present Old Rectory situated in Rectory Street. It was rebuilt within twelve months of the fire at a cost of £400). Much later, in 1724, Samuel would also be given the curacy of the nearby hamlet of Wroot, (where he and his family were to move for a period of seven years before returning to Epworth rectory) on the borders of Lincolnshire and Yorkshire. Meanwhile, he soon began his work amongst the parishioners but realised that the Islonians of Epworth were, in the main, rather a rough, aggressive and uneducated community. Nevertheless, he set about preaching, visiting the poor and sick, and establishing classes to educate the children of the parish. Susanna took care of the running of the home and education of their children. As each year went by, it was marked by another pregnancy for Susanna and the family continued to grow (she was to bear nineteen children in total, ten of whom survived childbirth into adulthood).

As the family became larger, so did the demands on Samuel's income in order to clothe and feed their offspring. His wife was thrifty, cautious in her use of money and equally strict with her children. Accordingly, they were trained 'to cry softly and fear the rod'. In addition, they were taught to ignore anyone or anything in the outside world – especially the local townsfolk who resented their father and his condemnation of their sins from the pulpit. Susanna taught her children in the schoolroom and each child was expected to learn the alphabet by their fifth birthday. Reading began on the following day and subjects ranged from standard classics to the Bible.

The family was beset by financial problems and on one occasion Samuel was arrested and sent to jail at Lincoln Castle (C24) because he was unable to clear a debt of thirty pounds. Although his annual income as rector of Epworth amounted to two hundred pounds, he was a poor manager as far as money was concerned. It was therefore left to Susanna to try and keep track of all outgoing monies. She had a thankless task on her hands. Whilst he was in Lincoln jail, Susanna sent some of her rings to her husband in an effort to try to pay off the debt. Samuel returned them forthwith and sent a letter appealing to the Archbishop of York with whom he was acquainted. He was not disappointed and the Archbishop helped towards his release. He later paid the family a visit at Epworth and gave them financial help towards paying off their debts.

In the main, despite their difficulties, the marriage was a happy one and undoubtedly the moral stance and Christian teachings of the parents had a profound affect upon their children. Samuel was a strict disciplinarian who could be uncompromising and unbending with his children. Susanna was a more gentle soul but, with a large family to teach and organise, would have insisted on teamwork within her regime in the home. However, there was one particular time when the couple violently disagreed with one another. Samuel noticed that at both morning and evening prayers, Susanna did not say 'Amen' when the King was mentioned. This was because she did not agree with William of Orange being King when his wife, Mary, who had the better claim, was dead. She felt he was not of Royal blood and therefore a usurper. On the other hand, Samuel was a strong Protestant and fully supported William. It led to a bitter row between Susanna and him. Samuel declared 'he could no longer share a bed with her' and in a fit of temper rode off on his horse to London!

In 1702, Samuel returned to Epworth for a reconciliation. The accession of Queen Anne, an anointed Queen, also took place that year which created a climate for the renewal of the relationship. A few months later Susanna became pregnant again. Their fourth son and fifteenth child, John, was born on 17 June

1703 (This date is in the 'old style' calendar. In the 'new style' – when the Gregorian Calendar was adopted in 1752 to align with European countries – the 17th became the 28th. Afterwards, John Wesley always celebrated his birthday on 28 June.) John was only the second son to survive (Susanna had earlier lost two baby sons) but was joined four years later by younger brother Charles on 18 December 1707. He was destined to become perhaps the greatest hymn writer of all time.

Although the Wesley sons are the best known of the family, one should not underestimate the range of talents shared between the seven surviving daughters whom history books have tended to overlook. All were very different in personality, six of them married and, between them, they were to experience their own fair share of problems. In a later age, it is reasonable to assume that some might have gone on to academic success like their brothers. In 18th century England, however, only sons were promoted in this way. Samuel and Susanna therefore concentrated on preparing Samuel Jnr, John and Charles for distinguished careers – most probably in the Church.

During a later absence of Samuel's in London in 1712, a curate was appointed to take over some of his duties in and around the parish of Epworth. This did not work out satisfactorily and the local parishioners were unimpressed with the new curate. The congregation at the parish church began to dwindle rapidly. This worried Susanna and she began to hold prayer meetings and worship in her own kitchen at the rectory on Sunday evenings. News of this soon spread and, in addition to her own family and servants, others asked if they could join in. The numbers soon rose to a total of two hundred people. In retaliation, the curate contacted Samuel in London, pointing out what was taking place and, in turn, Susanna received a letter from her husband instructing her to cease the practice of worship in the rectory forthwith.

Determinedly, she replied to Samuel stating that she felt she was completely in the right and, if he still maintained his stance, they would both answer 'when you and I shall appear before the great and awful day of Judgment'. He could not disagree.

Samuel was a kindly rector and worked hard in his efforts to help the people of Epworth during his ministry with them. Yet 'old habits die hard' and the antagonism and anger against him and his King persisted.

One evening during the winter of 1709 a fire broke out at Epworth Rectory. It was thought to be an act of arson by one of the local townsfolk venting his anger at the parson. The fire soon caught hold of the building and efforts were quickly made by Samuel and Susanna to evacuate the house with their family. They thought that all of the children had escaped the blaze when, suddenly, a little voice was heard from an upper window. It was that of young John. The thatched roof was blazing rapidly and almost on the point of collapse. Hurriedly, Samuel tried to get back into the house but to no avail.

Someone then had a flash of inspiration and ran forward grabbing one of his companions. He then climbed onto the shoulders of the other and reached upwards to the open window. He was just able to snatch young John away to safety as the roof began to collapse. In their great joy and relief, Samuel, Susanna and other members knelt down to thank God for sparing the life of the five-year-old infant. It was at that point that Susanna described him as 'a brand plucked from the burning' and felt that God had saved him for a purpose.

Though they had lost their home the family still remained intact and Susanna went about her work and the education of her children – especially young John – with renewed vigour. Furniture, books and papers had all been destroyed in the blaze and temporary accommodation for the family had to be found until a new rectory could be built. At quite an early age John showed firmness of character and by the time has was eight he had experienced his first communion.

The Old Rectory there today is the second and replaced the original after the fire of 1709. However, much restoration work on the building has been carried out over the years. After the Wesleys left, it remained the home of subsequent rectors of Epworth until 1954 when the World Methodist Church purchased it. Three years later, it was first opened to the public as a monument to the development of world Methodism. It is a registered museum and place of pilgrimage for people from all over the world and affectionately known as the 'birthplace of Methodism'.

The Old Rectory, built in the Queen Anne style, was the Wesley family home until 1735. Although rather a rambling house, it is full of character and interest giving a good insight as to what life might have been like in the days of the Wesleys. The motto above the front door reads 'To us the duty, to others the use, to God the Glory' – very apt for its many visitors. On entering the spacious Entrance Hall, the beautiful wooden sideboard, once owned by the Wesleys, catches the eye. After Samuel's death it was sold to the nearby Red Lion Inn in Epworth where it remained for a century before disappearing. It was rediscovered at a house in Cheshire and acquired when the Rectory was being restored. Also in the entrance area is a portrait of Susanna as a young girl in London and an interesting 'grandmother' clock. It once belonged to John and spaces between the Roman numerals are divided into four. These mark

*The Old Rectory, Epworth*

the quarter hours – for the clock once only had an hour hand. The fireplace in the entrance area contains bricks which were recovered from the shell of the original rectory.

Up the stairway is the Period Room, once used by Samuel and Susanna as their bedroom and which she often used for prayer and quiet meditation. Nearby is Samuel's Study and above the fireplace are the words of a hymn he wrote: Behold the Saviour of mankind. Another point of interest is a row of pegs in a wall cupboard. On these pegs Samuel hung his wigs which were seldom washed but freshened with powder. This was always done inside the cupboard to prevent powder spilling over into the Study. The nearby Keel Room has a beam which once formed part of a ship's keel. It includes a display of paintings and drawings connected with events from Methodist history. Moving on, at the top of the house is what is known as 'Old Jeffrey's Chamber'. It is reputedly haunted by the 'Wesley ghost'.

The story started in December 1716 when the Wesley family heard strange noises coming from the room. The breaking of glass was also heard. On checking the authenticity of the story, John was convinced it was true, though it was something beyond the family's past experience. The disturbances continued for nearly two months and his sisters then nicknamed the poltergeist Old Jeffrey. It suddenly disappeared in the following year but the legend has remained. Returning to the ground floor, the Kitchen is of special interest as it was in here that Susanna held her famous Sunday evening meetings whilst Samuel was away in London. A dining table is set out with pewterware plates and vessels together with other kitchen utensils. Of all the rooms in the house, this is the one which appeals to most visitors. Next door is Susanna's old schoolroom where she gave lessons to her children for six hours every day. It is now used as a gift shop. On leaving the Old Rectory, take a few moments to see the gardens. They are especially colourful in early spring when daffodils first burst into flower or in summer when the roses are in bloom.

On reaching the age of eleven, it was decided that John should leave Epworth for a full time education and he was sent to Charterhouse School (A7) in London where his elder brother, Samuel Jnr, was already a tutor at Westminster School. (His younger brother, Charles, was to leave for the same school at Westminster four years later.)

Samuel, their father, was also a poet and writer of hymns. He once published a commentary he wrote on the *Book of Job* but most of his work was destroyed in the fire of 1709. The Reverend Samuel Wesley died at Epworth in 1735 at the age of 72 and was buried in the churchyard of St Andrew's near to the south wall of the church. He had been Rector of Epworth for 39 years.

After he left for London and Oxford and during his travels, John Wesley was to make 34 visits to his home town. The first time, in 1742, was when he was refused the pulpit of St Andrew's by the Anglican rector. Instead, he preached to the assembled crowd in the churchyard from the top of his father's tomb as it was classed as private property and he could not be prevented from doing so.

Whilst in Epworth, the visitor should see the Red Lion Inn situated in the Market Place where John lodged during his visits in later years. It is a charming old coaching inn and in the Tartan Room is a picture of John Wesley. The inn is situated opposite the Market Cross from where he regularly preached. Also worthy of a visit is the Wesley Memorial Church which was built between 1888 and 1889 at a cost of £6,500. In 1882, the Wesleyan Methodist Conference had decreed that a church should be built in Epworth to the memory of John and Charles Wesley. It is an attractive building which stands back from High Street with an adjacent manse completed two years later. On entering the church, visitors usually admire the chancel arch and a beautiful stained glass window of the Risen Christ. It is surmounted by a roundel containing stained glass profiles of John and Charles Wesley copied from the J Adams memorial in Westminster Abbey. Encircling the images is a motif quoting John's famous words: 'Best of all is, God is with us'. Beneath the window is the communion table which originally served as an altar at St

Andrew's Parish Church and from it both Samuel and John administered Holy Communion. The carved oak font was a gift in memory of Susanna Wesley. (Almost opposite Wesley Memorial Church is a building, now a youth centre, which was the former church of the Methodist New Connexion sometimes known as Kilham Memorial Chapel after Alexander Kilham, its founder, who was born at Epworth in 1762. See also Chapter 10)

After his sheltered life in Epworth, John Wesley's departure for school in London was really the first opportunity he had had to see something of the outside world. His eyes were about to be well and truly opened.

CHAPTER 3

# Schooldays in London

YOUNG JOHN WESLEY's journey to London would most probably have been by coach. There is no doubt that a youth of such tender years would have been accompanied by either his father or elder brother, Samuel Jnr. who, earlier, had entered Westminster School, Dean's Yard, in 1704. Three years later, young Samuel had been nominated for election as a King's Scholar, an accolade which guaranteed free education and the strong possibility of a university place. He went on to Christ Church, Oxford, in 1711 and, having obtained his degree, returned to Westminster School to teach.

The route to London might well have been to Lincoln and then along the old Roman road of Fosse Way until such a place as it crossed the Great North Road from London to Edinburgh which ran a few miles to the west of Epworth. John must have felt apprehensive as he travelled towards the capital city. On the one hand, he was going on a new and perhaps exciting adventure. On the other, his earlier sheltered life back home at Epworth Rectory had hardly equipped him for what might lie in store. Certainly, he was morally aware of his responsibilities and had been told by his parents to 'put his faith in God'. No doubt brother Samuel would have tried to re-assure and encourage him about life in the city. Yet a boy not yet eleven years old must have had a few misgivings.

Apprehension would have probably turned to fascination as John reached London and saw for himself the bustle of people and noise in its busy streets. Perhaps he would have spotted a few famous buildings such as the newly-built St Paul's Cathedral (A1) by Sir Christopher Wren, and formally opened in 1697, erected to replace the earlier church after the Great Fire of London which started in Pudding Lane in 1666. Until then John would have only have seen such places in paintings or drawings. St Paul's dominated the London skyline surrounded by numerous other new churches and prominent buildings. What a change from the countryside where he had always lived. After the fresh north winds which blew across the Humber estuary and Lincolnshire flatlands he would have noticed in contrast the foul smells of the city's sewers and almost non-existent drainage systems. He would also have been struck by the poverty of many of its citizens and their dank crumbling houses huddled together in so much squalor. Indeed, it would all have come as somewhat of a shock to the lad.

John was nominated as a 'gown boy' at Charterhouse School by his father's patron who was also one of the school governors. A 'gown boy' was a pupil who received his education at no cost as long as he was nominated by one of the governors. He entered on 28 January 1714 and, at this time, wrote his surname as Westley. The site of Charterhouse already had quite a history.

It started life as a medieval Carthusian monastery in 1371 and was founded by Sir Walter de Manny, a distinguished soldier under Edward III. An original 14th century gatehouse is still intact on the north side of Charterhouse Square. The name Charterhouse is a corruption of the French Chartreuse which was the location of the first Carthusian monastery in the Middle Ages. However in 1537 it ceased to house the religious order during the Dissolution of the Monasteries by Henry VIII by which time many monks had been martyred. In 1545 the property was granted to Sir Edward, later Lord North, who built a mansion on the site incorporating materials from the former monastery. It was sold to the Duke of Northumberland who was put to death in 1553 as a result of his part in the plot to put Lady Jane Grey on the throne. Lord North once more took over the house and entertained Elizabeth I here prior to her coronation in 1558. Likewise, James I was also entertained there after his accession in 1603 by Thomas Howard, later Earl of Suffolk.

In 1611 the property was bought for £13,000 and taken over by Thomas Sutton, a wealthy soldier and merchant. He converted

*Charterhouse School*

it into a hospital for eighty poor pensioners and a charity school for fifty boys – called Charterhouse. (The original buildings still survive behind St Bartholomew's Hospital and provide a meeting place for the governing body and other gatherings.) The school provided an education for poor but scholarly youths who had been nominated by various sponsors – as indeed had John Wesley been. Other famous pupils have included Roger Williams, founder of Rhode Island in the USA; William Makepeace Thackeray, writer and novelist; and Robert Baden-Powell, founder of the Boy Scout movement. In 1872, the school – which had by then become a boarding school for fee-paying boys – transferred to Godalming in Surrey.

Subsequently, the premises in Charterhouse Square became a home for elderly gentlemen, mainly with either a military or professional background. On the north side of the Master's Court is the 16th century Great Hall which has a gallery and Renaissance screen. There is also a Great Chamber with an exquisite chimneypiece and fine carved ceiling. To the west is a place known as Washhouse Court – for obvious reasons – and to the north are more modern extensions. In the Great Cloister – around which the school boys would run – there are traces of original cells and a doorway used by the monks. What was originally the chapter house is now the Chapel, some of which dates back to the 14th century. This includes the fine tomb of Thomas Sutton, founder of Charterhouse. A plaque commemorating the links with John Wesley is situated in the nearby Chapel Cloisters. To allow public access, the buildings are usually open on Wednesday afternoons between the months of April and July. Entrance is by the Gatehouse from Charterhouse Square. The square is one of the few places still left in London which is lit by gaslight.

Prior to leaving Epworth, young John had been told by his father that at Charterhouse he should take a morning run three times around the green in order to improve his constitution. In his diary John says 'From ten to fourteen I had but bread to eat and not great plenty of that – but I believe that so far from harming me – this formed the basis of lasting health'. He was quite right and was to live until the ripe old age of almost 88.

The boy did not find life easy at Charterhouse and, being quite small, may have been bullied by older scholars. Certainly, his elders would steal food from the younger boys. Yet John worked well at his lessons which included Greek, Hebrew and Latin. He also took a keen interest in modern languages, encouraged by Dr Thomas Walker. Mr Andrew Tooke was responsible for teaching mathematics and natural science (a subject that would interest John in later life). Despite the hardships at school, his mother's strict up-bringing and discipline would have stood him in good stead. He is known to have been popular with other boys and renowned for his talent for storytelling. Two years after John entered Charterhouse, his younger brother, Charles, joined Westminster School as a scholar and later became Head Usher. It was around that time that the 'strange disturbances' were taking place at the Old Rectory between 1716-17.

At the age of seventeen, after a sound education at Charterhouse School, John left for Oxford. He had been awarded a scholarship of £40 per year and it was to set him on the road to a promising future. A new chapter in his life was about to begin.

# CHAPTER 4

# Oxford and the Birth of Methodism

'THE DREAMING SPIRES' of Oxford and its University would have proved quite a change for John Wesley after the closed confines of Charterhouse School and its surroundings. His parents had been delighted and proud that their second son had won for himself a place at such a prestigious place of learning. It appeared he was about to follow in both his father and elder brother's footsteps. John was elected a scholar of Christ Church on 24 June 1720 and matriculated on 18 July. His studies as an undergraduate had begun. The University's prime role at that time was to prepare young men to join the ministry of the Church of England and an average of seventy per cent took up holy orders.

Entering Oxford the River Thames divides and passes behind the railway station where Isis Lock links the river with the Oxford Canal. Soon after, it is joined by the Cherwell. The character of the city has been molded by centuries of history but it was virtually ignored by the Romans who considered it both low-lying and unhealthy. However the Saxons regarded it as strategically important and the name of Oxford appears in the Anglo Saxon Chronicle of AD 912. Since the 12th century Oxford has grown as an intellectual centre and place of learning and its achievements are known throughout the world.

The idea for Christ Church was first mooted by Thomas Wolsey, Cardinal Archbishop of York. In 1524, he received permission from the Pope to dissolve the former priory of St Frideswide, founder of the original college and Oxford's patron saint who died in AD 727. (His shrine and tomb have been retained in Christ Church Cathedral). Later, he was also given sanction to suppress a number of monasteries to provide lands and money to found a college in Oxford. Consequently, in 1525 the foundation stone of Cardinal College was laid by the Bishop of Lincoln. At the same time Wolsey issued his foundation charter.

The new college was planned on an unprecedented scale at a cost of thousands of pounds. However, the Cardinal fell into disgrace with Henry VIII because of his inability to achieve a divorce with his Queen, Catherine of Aragon, so that Henry could marry Anne Boleyn. Work on the new college came to a halt and it was thought that the King might demolish work already completed. Eventually, in July 1532, it was re-founded as King Henry VIII College. Thirteen years later, a third change came about when the Cathedral, formerly based at the other side of the River Thames at nearby Osney, and the college were amalgamated to form The Cathedral Church of Christ in Oxford. It has been so styled ever since. The wonderful chapel is the mother church of the Oxford diocese and, together with its college, is the most splendid of all buildings of the University.

One enters the great quadrangle of Christ Church under the famous Tom Tower. This was designed and built by Sir Christopher Wren in 1682 and contains the great bell Old Tom which was transferred from Osney Abbey and later re-cast. It still tolls 101 strokes every night from 21.05 hours (to commemorate the original number of undergraduates plus one added by a bequest – this was the time students had to be back in college). Walking around the quadrangle to the right, we re-enter college buildings and ascend an imposing staircase (built by James Wyatt in 1805 and used as a location in the recent Harry Potter films) to the magnificent Hall. It is the largest pre-Victorian college hall in either Oxford or Cambridge and has a decorated roof with over six hundred motifs. There are many portraits of the great and good on all four walls, each of whom had close links with the college, including fourteen British prime ministers. Notable are rare portraits of Cardinal Wolsey, painted by Sampson Strong in 1610, and Henry VIII, thought to be by the distinguished painter, Master John.

The portrait of John Wesley, painted in 1788 by George Romney, is also prominent. In addition are portraits in stained glass of both John and Charles Wesley high up in the second window to the right from entering the main door of the Hall. Other former students of Christ Church depicted include William Penn, the Quaker founder of Pennsylvania, who was sent down for Nonconformity in 1661. There is also the much revered Charles Lutwidge Dodgson (1852-1898) better known as Lewis Carroll, a distinguished mathematics scholar, and author of Alice in Wonderland and other children's books. The Hall has been the scene of many important and historic events. Elizabeth I watched a play, Charles I held a parliament here and even film star Charlie Chaplin once came to dinner.

John Wesley entered Christ Church in 1720 on a Charterhouse fellowship. At that time the college – and University in general – had developed a reputation for the loose living of its students. However, this does not seem to have distracted John in any way. It is reported he soon settled into his new surroundings and established a good rapport with his tutors, Henry Sherman and George Wigan. The new undergraduate was looked upon as rather a serious-minded but not unsociable student. He is known to have become involved with other college activities such as tennis, chess, reading and dancing and, occasionally, consorted with the opposite sex without forming any serious relationships. Within four years he achieved a Bachelor of Arts degree. After graduation, John continued at Oxford to study for a Master of Arts degree and eventually to go on for ordination as a priest. On 19 September 1725 he was ordained as a deacon by John Potter, Bishop of Oxford, in Christ Church Cathedral. Wesley's first sermon was preached shortly afterwards at St Mary's Church in Fleet Marston, isolated on a hillock two miles (3 km) west of Aylesbury in nearby Buckinghamshire, just off the A41. The church is concealed behind a circle of trees, the village it served having long disappeared. Built of stone in the 12th century, it consists only of a nave, chancel and porch. However, the interior is charming with a beautiful chancel arch rebuilt in the 14th century and the building is administered by the Churches Conservation Trust.

Christ Church Cathedral is unique. Not only is it the smallest and one of the most beautiful of English cathedrals but it is also a college chapel. Its origins go back more than a thousand years to Saxon times and it became an Augustinian priory in the 12th century. An ambitious rebuilding scheme got under way around this time which led to the layout of the present church, chapter house and cloisters. The nave, chancel and aisled transepts were also built culminating in the cathedral spire, thought to be one of the first ever built in England. All periods of English Medieval Gothic are represented in this lovely building and it was only in the late 19th century that the western end, walled off and built up by Cardinal Wolsey, was reconstructed and opened up to give access to the main quadrangle of the college. Around the same time the east end of the choir was re-built. The church is one where the visitor needs to linger to admire its many ornate features or, if fortunate enough, listen to the world-famous choir who sing regularly at daily services. It is quite an experience.

On 25 March 1726, John was elected as a Fellow of Lincoln College, Oxford, which delighted his parents. 'Wherever I am, my Jack is a Fellow of Lincoln!' his father is reported to have exclaimed with great pride. The post carried a yearly income and the right to a set of rooms in the college at no rent. These advantages would certainly have helped John's financial situation (which, in turn, would also have helped his family who were then living at Wroot near Epworth). The Fellowship was awarded under a special scheme for those born in Lincolnshire and was one of only twelve in the college. On 7 November he was chosen Greek lecturer and moderator of the classes, which increased his stipend. (George I died in the following year and was succeeded by his son as George II.)

The charter for Lincoln College was granted in 1427 by Henry VI and the college was founded by Richard Fleming, Bishop of Lincoln. He endowed his college of 'The Blessed Mary and All Saints Lincoln' with revenues of three local churches. The front quadrangle is one of the most attractive in Oxford with walls festooned with red creeper, especially colourful in early autumn.

It is entered from Turl Street. These and most other buildings date from the 15th century. Especially impressive is the perfectly-proportioned Hall which has remained a main common room as well as the dining room. It is the oldest surviving college hall in Oxford to retain its original 15th century roof. Well worth a visit are the library, kitchen and chapel. The Chapel, beautiful in appearance with some of the finest painted glass windows in Oxford, dates from 1631 and the stalls and ceiling from 1686. At the east end is a glorious window and six carved figures. The Chapel also has beautiful woodwork and a vaulted roof complete with armorial bearings, and the pulpit from which John Wesley preached is also on view. It is home to another highly successful choir.

In 1926, to celebrate the 200th anniversary of John's admission to his Fellowship at Lincoln College, a bust of the former Fellow was erected on a wall in the front Quadrangle and a room known as the Wesley Room restored to its original appearance. This however is not the room which John occupied. His actual rooms overlooked the Chapel Quad. The college is open to the public every afternoon.

By 1731 John and Charles Wesley started the practice of conversing with each other in Latin, a practice they were to maintain throughout their lives. From early years John had worn his auburn hair in long locks to shoulder length which, of course, turned whiter as the years progressed. He was small in stature and slim and with a fresh complexion and bright, piercing eyes.

Strangely enough, Methodism in Oxford took root in the town rather than the University and John Wesley was later to preach in the town centre in 1768. The following year he was not allowed to preach at the Dissenting Meeting House, now the New Road Baptist Chapel. As an alternative, he preached in the garden of the house of John Mears, a long-standing friend. By 1775 there were 530 members in the Oxfordshire Methodist circuit and a meeting house was built, now 32 and 34 New Inn Hall Street (on which a wall plaque has been erected) where Wesley preached on 14 July 1783 and again in the following year to a packed room. His last

visit to Oxford was on 29 October 1789. A later Methodist chapel was built in 1815 on the site of the present St Peter's College. It was replaced by a later building, the Wesley Memorial Church, which has an elegant spire, and opened on 11 October 1878. It continues to play an important role for Methodism in the life of the University city.

Meanwhile, younger brother Charles Wesley had, in 1721, become a King's scholar at Westminster School and was later appointed head boy. Like John, he also was elected a scholar of Christ Church and moved to Oxford in 1726. However, by that time John had moved on to nearby Lincoln College. Nevertheless, the two brothers saw much more of each other than they had in the previous years since each had left home. Charles initially intended to enjoy life at college and make the most of his student days, stating he was in no hurry to be 'made a saint'.

John gained his MA in 1727 and was ordained a priest in the following year on 22 September 1728 by Bishop Potter in Christ Church Cathedral. It was when he was at Lincoln College that he began to concentrate more on self-discipline. Around this time the Reverend Samuel Wesley Snr was taken ill and requested that John be given leave of absence from Oxford to help him as curate in his parish work at Wroot. John acted as curate between August of that same year and November 1729. It was over two years before he returned to Lincoln College to resume his responsibilities. Wesley was eventually summoned back to Lincoln College by Dr Morley, the Rector, to act as a tutor. The original church of which John was in control at Wroot has now disappeared and been replaced by a brick building. A Wesleyan chapel, built in 1870, stands in the quiet village but six miles walking distance from Epworth.

Charles matriculated at Christ Church in 1726 and began to take more interest in spirituality. When John returned in 1729, he found Charles a more sober person who had started to meet with other like-minded students to study the Bible, discuss religious subjects and social problems, to pray and, in general, persuade others to join them. They started to visit poor people in the town and prisoners based at both the town's Bocardo jail, which stood in Cornmarket Street until 1772, and at Oxford Castle.

Oxford Castle was built by Robert d'Oilly in 1071. Parts of the castle have survived including St George's Tower, the base of the Round Tower and the Mound. The prison, situated behind County Hall, was closed in 1996 but plans are in hand to refurbish the buildings in a partnership between heritage and commercial uses. The group of cells thought to have been visited by the Wesleys should once more become accessible to the public on completion of the project.

By 1730 Charles had become a tutor and John began to take a great interest in the activities of a group of students assembled by his brother. They started out studying the Greek Testament and attending the Sacrament. John soon joined them and became their leader. It was not long before they came to the notice of other students who began to ridicule them. They were mocked and given nicknames such as the Holy Club, Bible Moths, Sacramentarians and Methodists. Prior to his ordination John started to keep a diary in which he recorded how he spent his time and money every day. He also took note of any sins he committed. Members of the Holy Club also began to put aside some of their income to share with other less privileged members of society to help buy clothing, food and medicines. They also started to celebrate the Sacrament on a weekly basis (the norm for this in most parishes was only three or four times per year).

## George Whitefield

In 1732, Charles invited a new student to join the group. His name was George Whitefield, and was the youngest of seven children. He was born at the Bell Hotel in Gloucester (E25) where his father was an innkeeper and wine merchant. Sadly, his father had died when he was two and his widowed mother had struggled to keep family and home together. She re-married but it was not a success. When he was ten years old, the boy suffered a bout of measles which left him with a permanent cast in one eye.

Two years later, he started at St Mary-de-Crypt grammar school in Gloucester and was regularly reported for playing truant. It was at this school where he first developed a talent for acting and public speaking. As a family the Whitefields worshipped at St Mary-de-Crypt Parish Church where George had been baptized and grown up. By the age of fifteen he wanted to leave school and managed to persuade his mother to allow this. For a while he spent time working in the inn as a pot boy and bar tender but, at the back of his mind was an urge to preach. He started to study the Bible in earnest. Encouraged by an Oxford student who had gone there under similar circumstances, George set his sights on following a similar course. He returned to school to study for an Oxford education, achieved success and won a place at Pembroke College. He was later introduced to John and Charles Wesley. George Whitefield would, one day, have a profound influence upon the lives of both Wesleys, and vice versa.

Charles lent him a book to read – *The Life of God in the Soul of Man* – which caused George to really examine his spirituality and lifestyle at Oxford. This led to his conversion to Christianity in 1735 after which, due to ill health, he returned home to recuperate. Yet, despite his illness, he carried on with his activities at University and soon attracted the attention of Dr Benson, Bishop of Gloucester. Thoroughly impressed with the undergraduate, he agreed to ordain Whitefield as a deacon. By March of 1736, George was back in Oxford and on 20 June was ordained by Dr Benson. His first sermon was preached at St Mary-de-Crypt on the following Sunday but he was back again at Oxford by the following Wednesday when his BA degree was conferred upon him.

* * *

The Holy Club continued with their strict rules of study and religious observance under John Wesley and became known as the Oxford Methodists – the name that was to live on into the future. John always considered the Holy Club to have been the birth of Methodism. Yet they were not such a sanctimonious group as many would believe. John and Charles, though very different in temperament, are known to have had cheerful personalities endowed with much good sense and knowledge of human nature.

As well as preaching in Christ Church Cathedral, John also preached many times and took Communion in the University Church of St Mary the Virgin – the University church – though not from the existing pulpit. On seven occasions he was invited to give the annual University sermon. The church, one of the city's best-known landmarks and situated in the High Street, has the best of Oxford's gracious spires and towers. It also has a magnificent Renaissance-style porch with twisted 'barley-sugar' shaped pillars and a statue of the Virgin Mary and Child which was added in 1637. Views from the church tower are the finest in the area across what seem to be myriad spires and pinnacles.

It was in this church that the trials of the Protestant Archbishop Thomas Cramner and Bishops Nicolas Ridley and Hugh Latimer took place. The trials – during the reign of the Catholic Mary Tudor in September 1555 – first started in the 15th century Divinity School but moved to the nearby University Church. The three clerics defended their beliefs and opinions about the Eucharist. However, it was a foregone conclusion that they would be proved guilty and their statements condemned. Ridley and Latimer were burnt at the stake whilst Cramner was later to suffer the same fate. The Church of St Mary the Virgin still bears the marks of the scaffold. In 1841, a Martyrs' Memorial was erected in honour of the three Protestants at the site where they died. It is situated in Broad Street – once the town ditch – in front of Balliol College. An ornate cross set in the middle of the road marks the spot.

By 1735 John Wesley had started to become disillusioned with the Holy Club and its impact upon his own and other peoples' lives. His father had wanted him to succeed as rector of Epworth but John had no wish to return to the wilds and confines of Lincolnshire. For some time he had toyed with the idea of becoming a missionary and news filtered through about opportunities opening up for evangelism in the newly-founded colony of Georgia in North America. Perhaps there he would find the spiritual satisfaction he was seeking.

A few months later, an invitation came to both John and Charles from General James Oglethorpe, founder of Georgia, whom they had met in the summer. The result was that he invited both brothers to join him in his work across the Atlantic. John was to serve as a parish priest in the main settlement of Savannah, founded by Oglethorpe in 1733, whilst Charles would become Secretary to the General. It sounded like the opportunity they had both been waiting for. On 14th October 1735, they took a boat from Gravesend bound for the New World. It was to bring disappointment, disillusionment and a few surprises for both of them.

# CHAPTER 5

# Georgia

GENERAL JAMES OGLETHORPE was of the opinion that both John and Charles Wesley exactly fitted his prototype of English clerics. In other words, he preferred those who were somewhat pious, a bit staid in their ways and with a firm foothold in the Established Church. Disregarding their earlier activities in the Holy Club, Oglethorpe outlined to the brothers just what was involved in becoming spiritual leaders in Savannah (G2). It would also provide a chance for them to work as missionaries amongst new settlers and American Indians. The prospect of both seemed attractive to the two brothers and they greeted the chance to go to Georgia with much enthusiasm. John wanted to save his own soul, being spiritually disillusioned and unfulfilled with his work in Oxford. It was no accident that his published Journal begins at this point.

John was 32 and Charles 28 when they set out across the Atlantic. From the outset, John emphasised he was more interested in converting the native Indians rather than English settlers. He was also seeking a path to greater holiness. On the other hand, Charles had been specially chosen to occupy the office of Secretary to General Oglethorpe, a post which had been initiated in a mandate by the trustees of Georgia.

## James Oglethorpe

James Oglethorpe, a close friend of the Reverend Samuel Wesley Snr, was born in London on 22 December 1696 and baptized the next day at St Martin's-in-the-Fields. He matriculated at Corpus Christi College, Oxford, on 8 July 1714 and by 1710 had obtained a commission in the British Army. In 1718, he succeeded to Westbrook, the family estate near Godalming, Surrey, and four years later became MP for Haslemere, a seat he was to hold for 32 years. He was also successful in persuading Parliament to reform the notorious debtors' prison system – perhaps having been partly encouraged by the earlier experience of his friend, the Rev Samuel Wesley Snr, at Lincoln Jail.

In June 1732, to provide an outlet or new opportunity for such debtors as well as blocking Spanish expansion north from Florida, he and nineteen associates obtained a charter for settling the colony of Georgia in America. This was the region lying between the rivers Savannah and Alatmaha, named in honour of George II, who gave Oglethorpe every encouragement. Early in 1733, the General left Deptford on the River Thames with 120 specially chosen pauper emigrants and reached Charleston (G1), South Carolina. By 12 February he had founded Savannah. An equally significant success was the establishment of friendly relations with the Yamacraw Indians which remained unbroken throughout his stay in the colony. It was the thirteenth and last colony to be founded in the New World. James Oglethorpe also set up its defences against Spain, constructing forts and providing military training. In 1734 he returned to England and acquired a new ruling banning rum and slavery in the colony. He also sought out men who could take care of the spiritual needs of his rough settlers. This is where his thoughts turned to John and Charles Wesley, sons of his long-standing rector friend, Samuel.

It was 6 February 1736 when the boat *Simmonds* carrying Oglethorpe and the two Wesley brothers landed on American soil. Their first landfall was a small uninhabited island called Peeper (now Cockspur) Island near Savannah, and John Wesley led everyone in a prayer of thanksgiving (a monument now marks the spot near historic Fort Pulaski). They were later taken by Oglethorpe in another boat to Savannah and John preached his first sermon on 7 March at the courthouse. Among other settlers was a group of Germans from the Moravian Church, another Nonconformist organisation. In mid-Atlantic, the little ship had been hit by violent storms and John Wesley had been terrified. This was disturbing to Wesley who began to question his own lack of faith, especially when he noticed all the Moravians were facing up to the experience with calmness and much bravery. John later questioned them about this and was told that none were afraid of death. He was deeply moved and shaken by their response and composure. At the same time he felt great remorse at his own lack of faith and sincerity. John was also much influenced by their hymn-singing.

## The Moravians

The Moravian Church originated in the ancient Czech homeland – originally Bohemia and Moravia – in the mid-15th century, following the martyrdom of Jan Huss, the reformer of religion in Bohemia, who was himself influenced by the writings of John Wycliffe. It was established in 1467 as the first Protestant and Reformed Church of Europe, with its own Church Order, Rule and Life, and expanded nationally up to the time of the Counter Reformation of 1620. In the 18th century a group from Moravia, fleeing persecution, settled in Germany and became known as Moravians under the leadership of Count Zinzendorf. It is a community which, despite many changes, attempts to fulfill the words of Christ: 'We have but one Master, Jesus Christ; and we are all brothers and sisters in Him'. The Moravian Church was recognised by an Act of Parliament in 1749, took an active part in the evangelical Revival, and was to have a formative influence upon the Wesleys.

\* \* \*

Not long after reaching Savannah John found life in the new settlement was hard and soon became embroiled in disagreements about how the place should be run. Many settlers took little notice of his rigid rules and regulations and generally looked upon him as a bit of a laughing stock. Neither did brother Charles take to his post as Secretary to General Oglethorpe at his residence at Fort Frederica (G6), St Simon's Island (G4) – one of the Golden Isles just off the coast of Savannah. For a start he did not have a good rapport with his employer. Neither were other colonists warming to Charles' far too strict approach to his work, nor did he recognise baptism by laymen (those other than ordained priests). It was not long before he found himself being used as a scapegoat as a result of malicious gossip between two women – a Mrs Hawkins and a Mrs Welch – who each confessed to him that they had enjoyed an adulterous relationship with the General. Quite untrue – but Charles was accused of spreading the rumour. Soon afterwards Oglethorpe ordered Charles back to England on the pretext of delivering dispatches to the Georgia trustees and board of trade back in London. Charles wanted to resign there and then. He left Georgia on 26 July 1736 in poor health and bound for a stormy crossing of the Atlantic. After delays at Charlestown and Boston, he finally landed at Deal in Kent on the 3 December. On his brother's advice he decided to return to Oxford but did not resign his post as Secretary to General Oglethorpe until 3 April 1738.

Meanwhile, John stayed on in Savannah despite his disappointment at Charles' early departure. After he left, John spent more time at Fort Frederica and its environs. His first hymn book was published in Charleston in 1737. He was also unhappy with his work as a parish priest amongst such an unruly band of former convicts and rough adventurers who continued to resent his approach. Nor did he have much opportunity to try and win over the souls of American Indians as he originally had hoped.

John's stay in the new colony was not without incident. He had perhaps rather foolishly become friendly with an eighteen year-old girl named Sophy Hopkey. She was a vivacious and seemingly virtuous girl who was the niece of Thomas Causton, the chief magistrate and storekeeper in Savannah. From Sophy's point of view, Wesley's standing and intellect made him extremely attractive. She was bedazzled by him. However, perhaps against his better judgment, John was flattered that a much younger woman was showering so much attention on him. It was to prove a recipe for disaster.

They met daily when she joined in devotions. John taught her French, and they prayed together. In the evening he read her selections from the works of various religious writers. The relationship deepened and thoughts of marriage started to fill John's mind. However, he could not decide what to do and pondered long over the situation. Eventually Sophy became tired of waiting for a decision and, in haste, married another suitor, William Williamson. The outcome of the affair caused much unrest amongst other settlers. Matters were brought to a head when, on one occasion, Wesley refused to admit Sophy to the Sacrament. Chaos broke out and a series of charges were levelled against him causing John to make a quick departure from the colony. John wrote in his Journal 'I came to convert the Indians, but, oh, who will convert me?' John arrived back at Deal (F25) on 1 February 1738 – totally dispirited.

Despite a disappointing stay in Savannah, there is a John Wesley statue in Reynolds Square. Facing the statue, the site of Wesley's parsonage and garden is to the left. Even though Wesley had no church building, the visitor should see Christ Episcopal Church on Johnson Square where he served as rector and established the first Sunday School in America. Continuing around Johnson Square to the right is the site where Wesley held his first service of worship, now the US Customs House. The site of the Town Hall where John held regular services is now the US Post Office at Wright Square on Bull Street.

As for General Oglethorpe, he was ordered to attack St

Augustine (G5) on the east coast of Florida when England declared war on Spain in 1739. It was soon clear that this was beyond his ability and resources. Despite this failure he later defeated the Spanish at the battle of Bloody Marsh on 9 June 1742 near Fort Frederica on St Simon's Island. Georgia's survival was at last assured. After an unsuccessful attempt on St Augustine's the following year, Oglethorpe was ordered back to England. He never to returned to the New World. Georgia was declared a colony of the British Crown in 1752. The General died on 30 June 1785 in his 89th year and is buried in the chancel of the parish church in the village of Cranham near Upminster in Essex.

Anyone interested in tracing the life and exploits of General Oglethorpe should visit Godalming Museum, Surrey. It houses an informative display on his early days in England, his life in Georgia, and his various military achievements.

John Wesley also visited the St Simon's Island area during his stay in Georgia. Although the experiences of the two brothers in America were difficult, they did establish a congregation on St Simon's Island which was later served by George Whitefield. Today it is known as Christ Episcopal Church (G7), Frederica, and the old military road walked by the Wesleys runs between the church and a Wesley Memorial Garden. Just outside the church stands an oak tree under which John Wesley once preached.

After the American War of Independence, cotton plantations were established on the island, and native live oak timbers were used for shipbuilding. The Hamilton Plantation, which was located in the grounds, later became the third largest lumber mill in the USA. In 1949, the South Georgia Conference of the Methodist Church purchased the site and turned it into a conference centre, naming it Epworth-by-the-Sea (G8) to commemorate the earlier visits by the two Wesley brothers. The Lovely Lane Chapel, constructed in 1880, is still in use and the largest Methodist Museum in the nation is also on the site. The approach from Brunswick (G3) on the mainland of Georgia is via the FJ Torras Causeway to St Simon's Island.

## Savannah

Savannah today is quite removed from the usual bustling American city and takes just under five hours' drive from Atlanta. It stands on America's eastern seaboard where it is still a busy seaport and played host to the yachting events for the 1996 Olympic Games. The place still has much 'old world charm' and preserves its heritage in what is known as the nation's largest urban historic district. It was built on a grid system and over one thousand buildings have been restored. Many families still occupy the many elegant 19th century mansions and town houses on the showpiece estate. Trendy waterfront shops and restaurants now abound especially on the Riverfront and City Market areas, where there are many speciality shops selling antiques, antiquarian books and other collectables. Savannah was also the location for many scenes in the award-winning Hollywood film *Forrest Gump*.

The city is also renowned for its splendid walking tours – particularly around the historic district. John, Charles and other early Methodists are commemorated in the Wesley Monumental Church in East Gordon Street. The building is of Gothic Revival architecture and was opened in 1868. Further information can be obtained from the Savannah Visitors Center in Martin Luther King Jr. Boulevard. Close by in the old Central Georgia railway station is the Savannah History Museum which charts the area's early days from the time when cotton was the largest industry. One of the signatories of the American Declaration of Independence, Button Gwinett, the first Governor of Georgia, is buried in the Colonial Park Cemetery. He was born in the Gloucestershire village of Down Hatherley in 1735. As a young man he lived in Wolverhampton (c37) for some years practicing as a merchant and, in 1757, was married at St Peter's Parish Church before moving to the New World eight years later.

\* \* \*

After his own exploits in Georgia, John Wesley finally arrived back in England at Deal on 1 February 1738, totally disheartened. For neither he nor Charles had a sojourn to the New World been much of a success. It was soon afterwards that both their lives were to make a dramatic change. Things would never be the same again and life was to take on a whole new meaning.

# CHAPTER 6

# The Aldersgate Street Experience

AFTER HIS RETURN from America John Wesley was devastated by a sense of failure. For four days he was at a loss as to what to do with himself. He kept turning over and over in his mind his experiences at sea and his admiration for the bravery and sincerity of the Moravian group during Atlantic storms. Charles experienced similar feelings of frustration after his own return from Georgia and came back a sick man. By that time elder brother Samuel Jnr had been appointed headmaster of Blundell's School in Tiverton (E8), Devon. After some thought both John and Charles decided they would make contact again with the Moravians to whom they were strongly attracted. Subsequently, they met up with Peter Böhler, a leading member of the sect who had just landed from Germany, and took him to Oxford. Böhler, a twenty-six-year-old Moravian, was shortly to leave for America and their meeting was the start of a lifelong friendship between the three.

On return to London John and Charles went along to a religious society on 1 May 1738 which had originally started in the house of James Hutton, another Moravian. The group became the first Moravian Church in Britain in 1662. By December 1738 they moved to occupy a room in Fetter Lane in the City and became known as the Fetter Lane Society. Two years later the Moravians moved again into a previously Nonconformist chapel also in Fetter Lane. A few months later John Wesley left the group to set up his own society at a derelict foundry wrecked by a bomb in 1716. It stood at the north-west corner of Moorfields and he bought it in 1739 for £115 (see Chapter 7).

## Moravian Close, Chelsea

The Fetter Lane building was later destroyed by bombing during the Second World War and the site is now commemorated by a wall plaque on a modern office building. The congregation moved to a new home at Chelsea called Moravian Close just off the busy King's Road area but set in a quiet backwater. Sadly the site is now overlooked by a multi-storey building. The land was once owned by Sir Thomas More, Chancellor to Henry VIII in the 16th century, along with other large estates in Chelsea – almost the entire parish west of Old Church Street; and from the River Thames to what is now the Fulham Road. His first house, the Farm House, on the site of which now stands Lindsey House, built in 1674, was quite modest. Later, a second palatial building was erected and became known as Beaufort House after the Duke of Beaufort who owned it in 1682. In 1750 Count Zinzendorf bought Lindsey House and its adjoining lands for what was envisaged as a settlement to be called Sharon. The burial ground – known as God's Acre – was laid out in typical Moravian style of four quarters; and the Chapel and Clergy house were built on the site of Sir Thomas More's stables. James Hutton, Peter Böhler and John Cennick are all buried in the cemetery along with other notable Moravians. The whole complex is known as World's End and is a gem of grace and peace. Visitors are welcome to see over the premises, permanent exhibition, and burial ground which are open on Wednesday afternoons.

When I visited, I caught the London underground to Sloane Square then the No.11 bus along the busy but still trendy King's Road in Chelsea and asked to be put off at the Blue Bird Club. Just around the corner in Milkman Street I stepped through a wicket gate into Moravian Row. It was like stepping back in time!

\* \* \*

John poured out his heart to Böhler as to how his life seemed full of void despite his background and training as an Anglican priest.

He felt very much at a crossroads in life and thought that, without the necessary faith in God, he should give up preaching. Peter Böhler, his spiritual adviser, suggested: 'preach faith till you have it; and then, because you have it, you will preach faith'. In other words, a clear sense of assurance of salvation could only be achieved by having proper faith. This seemed like sound advice. The brothers thought long and hard about the words of wisdom they received from the Moravians at their small, intimate meetings. In consequence, they started to learn the German language.

## Aldersgate Street

Charles Wesley was the first to experience the 'feeling' of re-assurance which Böhler had explained to them. He was at the time recovering from an illness at the house of John Bray, another Moravian, who lived in Little Britain, Aldersgate Street (the present building has a blue plaque). Bray was described as 'a poor ignorant, who knows nothing but Christ'. On Whit Sunday, 21 May 1738, as Charles was falling asleep, he overheard Bray's sister say to someone – 'In the name of Jesus of Nazareth, arise, and believe, and thou shalt be healed of all thy infirmities.' These words immediately struck a chord with Charles and soon felt himself at peace with his Maker. John Bray said that this was a message from Christ himself. Charles is quoted at the time as saying, 'I felt a strange palpitation of heart. I now found myself at peace with God, and rejoiced in hope of loving Christ. I said, I believe, I believe.' Referring to his brother, John Wesley writes in his Journal that, 'His bodily strength returned also from that hour.' This event in his life has thereafter been marked as Charles' conversion.

John went to see Charles that evening and learned of his news. He rejoiced for his brother's sake and they sang and prayed together. Nevertheless, he must have felt dismayed that he did not feel the same way himself. Prior to his conversion, Charles spotted a text which, in his own case as a musician and writer of hymns, was to prove more than prophetic. It said 'He hath put a new song in my mouth, even a thanksgiving unto our God'.

Three days later John underwent a similar experience which would not only change his own life but very soon begin to change the face of England. The event took place at a small religious society meeting held at a house in Aldersgate Street to which he was invited by his Moravian friend, James Hutton. The building has now disappeared and the approximate site of the original house is in Nettleton Court at the main entrance to the Museum of London (A4). (Old Nettleton Court was an alleyway running from the street – between inns and houses to an orchard beside the Bastion in the City Wall, which still remains. The modern Nettleton Court runs parallel to and just south of the historic line of Wesley's day, but at high walk level.) This is known as John Wesley's Conversion Place and a modern bronze sculpture, known as the Aldersgate Flame, has a facsimile of Wesley's Journal for Wednesday 24 May 1738, which reads:

'In the evening I went very unwillingly to a society in Aldersgate Street, where one was reading Luther's preface to the *Epistle to the Romans*. About a quarter before nine, while he was describing the change which God works in the heart through faith in Christ, I felt my heart strangely warmed, I felt I did trust in Christ, Christ alone, for salvation; and an assurance was given me that he had taken away my sins, even mine, and saved me from the law of sin and death.'

Of that day, Charles Wesley wrote of his older brother, John, 'Towards ten, my brother was brought in triumph by a troop of our friends and declared *I believe!*'

\* \* \*


The Museum of London depicts the long history of the great metropolis and the 18th Century Gallery houses a bust of John Wesley and other items of memorabilia connected with early Methodism along with the Wesleys' and Whitefield's London.

## St Paul's Cathedral

John Wesley also worshipped in the Chancel of nearby St Paul's Cathedral on Wednesday to Friday, 24 - 26 May 1738. This is an area of the great cathedral not normally open to the public but groups are admitted on special occasions. In the north-west corner of the churchyard is a statue of John Wesley erected in 1988. It is a bronze cast of an earlier 19th century marble statue by Manning which stands in the Methodist Central Hall in Westminster.

St Paul's Cathedral was built between 1675-1710 following the Great Fire of London in 1666 when the original medieval building was left in ruins. The authorities invited Christopher Wren to rebuild it but he met with much opposition. On entering, the visitor notices the cool, orderly but very spacious interior. The nave, transepts and choir are shaped in a cross and crowned by the famous Dome, one of the largest in the world at 365 feet (111 metres) high, at the intersection of the arms. On the inside of the dome is the Whispering Gallery, where a whisper against the wall can be heard on the opposite side. Higher still is the Golden Gallery – 530 steps from the ground giving panoramic views over London. There is much evidence of fine Baroque architecture and decor in this beautiful cathedral which is regularly the setting for national and state events. Prominent are the monuments and caskets of Arthur Wellesley, first Duke of Wellington, and Admiral Lord Horatio Nelson, whilst that of Sir Christopher Wren himself is but a simple marble slab in the Crypt of his mighty masterpiece.

\* \* \*

During the following months, John had further meetings with the Moravians and other groups to explore spiritual and devotional life. These groups became known as 'societies' and were an extension of normal church activities. The idea would later be adopted by John as Methodist doctrines began to spread. At the outset and for some months thereafter, John and Charles preached from many London pulpits. Let us take a look around some of the better-known sites.

Firstly, St Giles's Parish Church, Cripplegate, in the Barbican area was mentioned earlier as the place from where Samuel Annesley, father of Susanna Wesley, was expelled for Non-conformity. The church was completed in 1550 and managed to survive the Great Fire in 1666. Oliver Cromwell was married in St Giles in 1620, and the poet John Milton, and Sir Martin Frobisher, the explorer, are both buried there. Sadly, the building was gutted by bombing in the Second World War but has since been lovingly restored. It was originally a chapel of ease to St Paul's.

The Church of St Bartholomew the Great in West Smithfield (A5) is the oldest parish church in the City, originally founded as an Augustinian monastery in 1123. John Wesley preached there on six occasions long after he had been debarred from other London churches for preaching Uniformity. The Lady Chapel was once occupied by a printing business and Benjamin Franklin, later to become the great American scientist and statesman, worked there as a youth in 1725. The church is approached through an ornate 13th century half-timbered gatehouse on the east side of Smithfield. This arch was once part of the church until the nave of the earlier building was pulled down at the Dissolution of the Monasteries. The gatehouse, which survived the Great Fire, now leads to a small graveyard. In the church are fine examples of Tudor tombs and the painter William Hogarth was baptized there is 1697. In recent times the building was the location for scenes from the award-winning film *Shakespeare in Love*.

Thirdly, St Luke's in Old Street (A12) was the parish church for the City Road area. It was built in 1732 and the place where John Wesley and his followers regularly went for communion, baptisms, marriages and burials. However, he did not actually preach there until 1778. In order that his own services at the nearby Foundery did not conflict with those at St Luke's, he held them at five o'clock in the morning and nine at night. The church has a most unusual obelisk on its clock tower and was once a large-galleried church with a high pulpit and magnificent altar. Sadly, due to subsidence, the building has been partly demolished and is now out of use. It can only be viewed from the outside.

\* \* \*

John Wesley continued to preach in parish churches with no variation from the established Order of Service but at society meetings started to use extempore prayer. His debt to the Moravians for the help they had given compelled John to visit Herrnhut in Germany, the headquarters of the Moravian church. It was here that in 1727 there had been an 'outpouring of the Spirit' which brought about a religious Revival of that Church. Wesley travelled through Holland, North Germany and eventually reached his destination on 1 August 1738. During his sojourn he attended a Bible Conference and went to church at Bertholdsdorf, a Lutheran village about a mile from Herrnhut (he refers to the town as Hernhuth in his Journal) and seems to have found his stay both fruitful and enjoyable. He also learned much: the importance of hymn-singing, the 'watch-night' service and the division of larger congregations into groups of four or five people – of the same sex and marital status – for the purpose of spiritual development. However, after spending some time with the Moravians, John began to question their kind of Christianity, thinking it a little too emotional and worldly. He stayed a fortnight and returned to London by 16 August. Herrnhut is about thirty miles (48 km) from Dresden and, in Wesley's day, was situated in Upper Lusatia, on the border of Bohemia.

Wesley began to spend more of his time with religious societies in both London and Bristol (E23) (where Nonconformism had already taken a hold) and began to recruit new people. On 21 October John and Charles met with Edmund Gibson, Bishop of London, and asked him whether, in his opinion, such religious groups were considered as Nonconformist. The Bishop doubted this and so John went up to Oxford and spent a month devising rules for the newly-formed societies. Despite the work he was doing, Wesley maintained the disciplines and teachings of the Anglican Church. However, he began to feel that God was leading him into aspects forbidden by the Church of England. This included preaching in a parish without first having obtained permission from the local priest. He reacted by claiming that as a Fellow of Lincoln College he was not bound by such rules. It was not long before he was to strike out in a completely new direction.

# CHAPTER 7

# Bristol and Bath

EARLIER IN 1738 George Whitefield had left for America on a mission similar to that of the Wesley brothers. He arrived in Georgia on 7 May but soon caught a bout of fever. Once having recovered, he set about his work and, unlike John and Charles, was encouraged by the response of both American Indians and British emigrants. In particular, he was greatly concerned with the plight of orphans and set up a girls' school in Savannah. This was his first visit to North America and he stayed four months before returning to London.

The following January, Whitefield was ordained a priest of the Church of England by the Bishop of Gloucester at a ceremony in Oxford. On his return to London George fully expected he would be welcomed by the various parish churches and invited to preach in their pulpits. This was not the case. His growing reputation for working with various religious societies and groups – especially those being set up by the Wesley brothers – began to anger the Established Church who saw it as a route to Nonconformity. Consequently, Whitefield soon found many churches were closed to him. There were still a few which allowed him to preach but, in the main, he concentrated on working with the Moravians in London, as they were not considered Nonconformist by Church of England authorities. More and more people were attending such meetings and over-crowding became quite a problem. Something had to be done.

News came to George that in Wales two other preachers – Howell Harris (1714-73) and Daniel Rowland (1711-90) – had begun to preach in the open air. It was a new idea and Whitefield wondered if he should do likewise. On consultation with John and Charles Wesley and other colleagues from the Holy Club in

Oxford he decided this would be his way forward. In February 1739, he left London for Bristol.

George Whitefield was charismatic and had a powerful preaching voice which was even admired by the famous actor, David Garrick (1717-1779). He developed into a dramatic and most effective preacher who often stirred his congregations. Whitefield first tried preaching in the open on 17 February in a coal-mining area known as Kingswood Hill just outside the city of Bristol. It was an area once covered by a Royal Forest in the Middle Ages but by the 18th century had become notorious for its squalor, crime, violence and poverty and was more or less avoided by local clergy. That someone like Whitefield should take the trouble to go among them certainly endeared him to the local workers and their families. Two hundred coal miners turned up to hear him and Kingswood Hill became a regular preaching spot. By his fourth meeting the congregation had swollen to as many as 10,000. Whitefield also had similar experiences in Bath (E22) and Cardiff (E28) and returned to Bristol at the end of March. Here, he was loaned a large field in the central area of the city where he preached to nearly 8,000 people. However, George had commitments both to go to London and for a return visit to America, so he invited John Wesley and another Moravian friend, John Cennick, to replace him at Bristol and Kingswood. Wesley arrived on the 31 March and observed Whitefield's preaching at the 'open field' site. He wrote in his Journal of the event 'I could scarce reconcile myself at first to this strange way of preaching in the fields, of which he [Whitefield] set me an example on Sunday: having been all my life so tenacious of every point relating to decency and order, that I should have thought the saving of souls a sin, if it had not been done in a church.'

On the following day, 1 April 1739, Wesley went with Whitefield to Hanham Mount where he heard his colleague preaching to the coal miners. The spot is significant in that it is the place where Methodist missionary work amongst the working classes, the poor and downcast really began. A week later, John preached there himself and continued to do so over many years.

The site is at Mount Hill Road, just east of the Kingswood to Hanham road, and was laid out as a public open space in 1951. It features a flagged cross marking the spot where field preachers such as Whitefield and Wesley once stood. The mount is topped by a beacon which sends out a green light over the surrounding countryside. A bronze plaque on the beacon commemorates that the two preached some of their earliest open air sermons close by. Eastwards from the beacon is a path leading to a replica of Wesley's school pulpit.

George also had another plan in mind – to open a school for miners and their children to educate them in Christianity. Before he left for America he set in motion a fund-raising scheme and on 2 April 1739 the foundation stone of a new school was laid.

John was especially keen on the school project but felt the chosen site was unsuitable. He set about acquiring an alternative between the Bath and London roads close to a place called Two Mile Hill – about three miles (4.8 km) from Bristol. He also started to raise more funding and made contact with various prominent people including Selina, Countess of Huntingdon, a keen supporter of the Methodist Revival. Within four months the schoolhouse began to take shape. By the end of a year the school was holding separate classes for boy and girl pupils with John Cennick as its first schoolmaster. The building also served as a preaching house for John Wesley's ministry.

By 1741, Wesley and Cennick had begun to disagree over school policy and so the latter began to build a rival school about a mile away in Park Road – which became known as 'Whitefield's Tabernacle'. Five years later, Wesley also decided to set up another institution as a boarding school for the sons of his preachers and other Methodist families. He felt that shielding young men from the temptations of the outside world in such a centre would better equip them to receive a proper Christian education. Wesley's New House was built on land adjoining the original miners' school and opened on Midsummer Day in 1748. The miners' school continued for some years in the original building, which also served as the new school's chapel and place of worship for the local Methodist society until 1844. His aim was to develop the school – Kingswood – into a college in which students could stay on for a further five years to acquire qualifications for the ministry. The original idea was abandoned until 1768 when Oxford began expelling students who were Methodists.

Kingswood School moved to the slopes of Lansdown, Bath (E22), in 1851. The original estate and buildings at Kingswood, Bristol, were disposed of and became a reformatory. All the buildings were demolished by 1917 but the pulpit was rescued and has been re-erected in the new school's dining hall. The Wesley Centre houses displays illustrating the origin and growth of the school including memorabilia from Wesley's day and models of the original building. Also of interest in the city is the Building of Bath Museum situated in the former Chapel of the Countess of Huntingdon in The Vineyards. It relates how Bath was transformed from a small provincial spa into a city of Georgian splendour within a period of one hundred years. The exhibition explores various crafts and personalities which contributed to Bath's development. The Chapel, which houses a 'Buildings' gallery, was commissioned by the Countess in 1765, as one of many chapels she was to have built as part of the Nonconformist Connexion. It is a beautiful Gothic building of the 18th century. The Schoolhouse, which houses the 'Interior' gallery, is adjacent to the chapel and built in the 1840s. In later years, John Wesley often preached in Bath and on one occasion in 1739 had a verbal encounter with Beau Nash, the well-known Regency dandy, at a site now occupied by the road of Palladian buildings known as the Circus. Wesley won the argument.

John stayed in Bristol for two months and always preached in the open air due to the fact that no church would offer him a pulpit. In May 1739 he bought a small piece of land in Bristol's Horsefair where he intended to build a room which could be used by the growing societies being formed from his new converts from the Anglican Church or earlier non-believers. Charles Wesley was initially unhappy with his brother's preaching in the open air but still supportive of what he considered was the work of God. After a few weeks John Wesley accepted a farmer's offer of the use of a field where a congregation of about five hundred people gathered to hear him preach. Charles was also preaching to larger numbers back in London at Newington Common and Moorfields (A8) though he would always first request the use of the nearest parish church beforehand. Working together, John and Charles were to become the joint leaders of the Methodist Revival and divided responsibility for Bristol and London between them.

However, many of the Anglican clergy disapproved of the way in which the Wesleys, and on many occasions their lay preachers, often preached in their parishes without permission. Hostility towards the Methodists began to build, especially against the small groups and class meetings where followers compared their spiritual life with one another. The Methodists were even accused of being papists and plotting to overthrow the Government (this was just a few years before Bonnie Prince Charlie's attempt to re-take the British throne on behalf of his father and the Catholic Stuarts).

## The 'New' Room, Bristol

On Sunday 3 June 1739 members of two Bristol societies met for the first time in the shell of what was to become known as the New Room. It became not only a centre for worship but also somewhere that John Wesley could train his lay preachers, introduce a dispensary for the sick, and also provide a book room. To raise funding to pay for the project, it was suggested that groups of twelve people should contribute one penny per week towards the cost. This was the forerunner of what is known in Methodism as the Society Class. These classes regularly met for prayer meetings and Bible study. However, the building soon proved too small to cope with the numbers of people involved in New Room activities and so plans were made to enlarge the building. This was not completed until 1748 when the building was licensed for public worship. The enlarged building included a chapel, accommodation for visiting preachers, rooms for John and Charles Wesley, and stabling for horses. For the remainder of his life, the New Room was the centre of John Wesley's activity in the South West and Wales and eighteen of his annual Conferences were held here, including the last in 1790. This was the forerunner of the Methodist Conference which still meets annually in late June at a series of locations around Britain.

The New Room (John Wesley's Chapel) stands in a quiet oasis off the busy shopping thoroughfares in Bristol city centre. An equestrian statue of John Wesley by sculptor A Gordon Walker overlooks the courtyard off Broadmead whilst a statue of Charles Wesley in preaching mode by Brook Hitch stands in the garden overlooking the Horsefair. Entering from the courtyard, one's attention is attracted to a single storey building with red pantiled roof, a small annexe to the right of the main building. This is the original building where itinerant preachers stabled their horses. Going into the chapel itself is like stepping back into history. Six stone pillars support the gallery and living quarters above the chapel. Prominent in the centre is the two-tier pulpit (lessons from

*'The New Room', Bristol*

the scriptures were read out from the lower deck whilst the preacher delivered his sermon from the upper). In front of this is the 18th century communion table at which John and Charles shared Holy Sacrament with their congregations. Notable in the balcony of the chapel are the long wooden forms which must have proved uncomfortable for the congregation when faced with a long sermon. The pews on the ground floor were not there in Wesley's time and congregations sat on forms similar to those in the gallery.

An unusual feature is that there is no direct access to the pulpit from the floor of the chapel. The route is via a staircase to the left-hand balcony close to the entrance doors and across to the other end of the building. An alternative approach is from the living quarters to the right of the pulpit which are reached by a back staircase. The clock on the side of the gallery was presented by John Wesley.

The original preachers' rooms and other living quarters contain much memorabilia of John and Charles Wesley as well as other prominent Methodist preachers such as Bishop Francis Asbury, Dr Thomas Coke, Adam Clarke, John Fletcher and Captain John Webb, who each have a room dedicated to their memory. There are many interesting paintings, drawings and other artefacts relating to the early days of Methodism. For Methodists and those interested in their history no visit to Bristol is complete without a visit to the New Room. It holds regular services, concerts and other events in the Methodist calendar.

## The Foundery Chapel, London

In June 1739 John Wesley rode back to London and started to preach in the open air as he had in Bristol. He began to set up societies which met weekly for prayer, discussion and worship under a lay-leader. On 16 July 1740 John found he was excluded from the Fetter Lane chapel and so withdrew from that society. It was to prove the start of his break with the Moravians. Instead, he managed to purchase for £115 a former cannon factory, a long-disused Government building in Windmill Hill (now

Tabernacle Street, Finsbury Square). It required another £700 spending on repairs, refurbishment and enlargement before it became habitable. John's intention was to use it as a preaching house – which would hold 1,500 people, create a centre for his own society, and also provide a home for elderly women, including his widowed mother, Susanna. For a generation the 'Foundery' building and chapel became the headquarters of Methodism in London until the City Road chapel (A10) was opened in 1778.

In 18th century England most turnpike roads radiated from London but, in 1730, a major development took place when a nation-wide turnpike system was introduced. Prior to this, few turnpike roads had been in existence and travelling to other parts of Britain was extremely difficult and fraught with problems. The new system meant that local parishes crossed by the new roads were responsible for covering any repair or maintenance costs within their own area. Two prime examples of this were the Great North Road beyond Northamptonshire and practically the whole of the Great West Road to Bristol. Turnpike trusts benefited from this injection of local funding with the security of a carefully graded system of tolls to produce income. John Wesley and his fellow preachers would undoubtedly have found improving travel conditions as new roads were constructed.

In the spring of 1741 John had to travel from London to Bristol and left a young man, Thomas Maxfield, in control of the Foundery. Because no priest was on hand to conduct services, Maxfield, though not ordained to do so, began to preach. Wesley found out about this, was angered by the news, and immediately returned to London. However, his mother was first to greet him with the words 'My son, take care what you do. Thomas Maxfield is as much called to preach the Gospel as ever you were!' She went on to suggest he listen to the young man in the pulpit. This he did – and was impressed. Thus, Maxfield became one of John Wesley's first lay preachers. By the close of the year Wesley had twenty more who were assisting his work in different parts of the country.

The former site of the Foundery (1738–78) is marked by a ceramic plaque on a wall in Tabernacle Street, about fifty yards (45m) south of Wesley's Chapel on the west side. It commemorates the first Methodist bookroom and also the death of Susanna Wesley on 30 July 1742. The original Foundery pulpit and some pews can be seen in the Foundery Chapel in Wesley's Chapel in City Road. The name 'Tabernacle Street' is derived from the original Moorfields Tabernacle (A11) built by George Whitefield in 1753 (it was dismantled in 1868 and replaced by a new church but is now used as a school).

\* \* \*

By 1742 the work of John and Charles Wesley was beginning to expand across the country. Later that year they both visited Newcastle-upon-Tyne (B20) – which they were to come to look upon as their 'Northern cornerstone' – working with the poor, new converts and helping train new lay preachers. Charles Wesley should never be under-rated, as he also was a powerful preacher and had the great gift of hymn-writing upon which much of Methodist worship has been based. Until Charles's marriage in 1748, the brothers often travelled around the country, together or separately, to preach the Gospel and organise Methodist societies.

Late in 1747 Charles made a trip to Ireland, returning there again the following August. It was through these visits that he first became acquainted with the family of Marmaduke Gwynne of Garth, Breconshire in South Wales (the original Gwynne family home is still known as Garth Brecon). His was a wealthy and staunchly Anglican family. In particular, Charles was attracted to his daughter Sarah, also known as Sally, and romance soon blossomed between the pair. At the time Sarah Gwynne (1726-1822) was 21 and Charles approaching forty. However, marriage to an itinerant preacher would not have formed the basis of a good partnership for any woman so John Wesley guaranteed his brother an income of one hundred pounds a year from the publication of Charles's hymns (this would be from income obtained by John and his preachers whilst on their travels through the sale of books of hymns and other religious material). It would mean the couple would be able set up home together so as to guarantee stability to the marriage.

Sarah and Charles were married by brother John Wesley in the nearby Llanlleonfel Parish Church (E34) on 8 April 1749. The wedding group was small and they walked across the fields from Garth House half a mile away. (It was reputedly in Garth House where Charles wrote the hymn 'Jesus, Lover of My Soul' in an upstairs room during a thunderstorm.) The site of Llanlleonfel Church dates back to early Roman times but the building fell into decline in the 18th century. It was rebuilt in the late 19th century and a plaque on the north wall commemorates the Wesley marriage.

## Charles Wesley's House, Bristol

Although Charles continued to travel, his journeys were no longer as extensive as those of his brother and soon, on 1 September that year, the newly-married couple set up home in Charles Street, Bristol. It was here that their children were born. Several died in infancy and are buried in the churchyard of the nearby St James's Parish Church, reputed to be the oldest in Bristol dating from Norman times. The three surviving children each proved to be gifted in some way. Daughter Sally had literary talent whilst brothers, Charles Jnr (1757-1834) and Samuel (1766-1837) were both gifted musicians. (Samuel became a child prodigy as a composer and performer though his efforts were later superseded by his own brilliant son, Samuel Sebastian Wesley (1810-1876), the distinguished composer and cathedral organist). The area around Charles Street was then part of a high class residential district and the family lived there until 1771 when they moved to London. No. 4 Charles Street, where they lived for at least part of the time, is a typical Georgian three-storey town house, recently restored and arranged as it might have appeared in the Wesleys' time.

Visitors can see the parlour, kitchen, music room and garden as well as an exhibition room, and the study where Charles wrote many of his seven thousand hymns.

\* \* \*

The legacy of training preachers for the ministry still continues in Bristol at Wesley College in College Park Drive, Henbury Road, which has a library containing Wesleyana and three thousand pre-1851 books together with pamphlets and tracts relating to early Methodist controversies. It is open to the public from Monday to Friday.

After the New Room was established in Bristol, both John and Charles began to accelerate their work of itinerant preaching and organised further societies in other parts of Britain. From hereon we shall be looking at specific regions, highlighting both events and locations which played an important part in their individual stories. It was not an easy task they had taken on and they met regular opposition not only from the Establishment but also from violent and demonstrative crowds of people. The brothers were to need every ounce of faith and courage to see them through.

# CHAPTER 8

# Birmingham, Black Country and the Wednesbury Riots

JOHN WESLEY FIRST passed through Birmingham (C40), now part of the West Midlands, and dined there in March 1738 on his way to preach in Stafford. He referred to Birmingham in his Journal as 'a barren, dry uncomfortable place'. On a later visit he preached in the Bull Ring area, on Gosta Green, and in a garret in Steelhouse Lane. By 1750 a Methodist meeting house had appeared at the corner of Steelhouse Lane and Whittall Street. This was burned down by a mob the following year. The congregation moved to a disused playhouse off Moor Street. In 1782, John preached there for the last time before opening a new chapel, which was to last another forty years before it was replaced.

Coventry (E37) is also in the same county and, on 21 July 1779, Wesley was due to speak in Cheylesmore Manor park but was prevented by heavy rain (only the medieval gatehouse of the estate still remains, off New Union Street). He duly asked the mayor of the town if he could use the town hall (the 14th century St Mary's Hall) in order to address the gathering. However, permission was refused in favour of a dancing master's class. John then proceeded to the women's market, which stood under the site of the present Leofric Hotel, off Broadgate, and preached to an attentive crowd on two consecutive days. He returned to London by coach from either the White Bear or King's Head Inns bound for the Cattle and Falcon hostelry in London's Aldersgate Street. Wesley was in Coventry again on 15 July 1782 and preached at the Cross House of the free grammar school which once stood at the junction of Priory and New Streets. The site is now occupied by the main entrance of the University of Coventry. Other visits to the town followed, the last being in 1787.

Charles Wesley and his colleague Charles Casper Graves were the first Methodists to visit the Black Country in September 1742 (the area was so called because of the black coal seam just below the earth's surface which was heavily mined up to the mid-20th century). It contains a series of townships lying mainly between Wolverhampton and Birmingham. For many years it was a heavily industrialised area encompassing such places as Dudley, Walsall, West Bromwich and parts of the city of Wolverhampton. As well as coal, the area was renowned for its metal-bashing industries and resources such as iron ore, limestone and wood for charcoal burning. An outstanding event in its industrial history occurred in 1712 when a Cornish engineer, Thomas Newcomen (1663-1729), erected his first pumping engine near Tipton in order to extract water from coal mines. Miles of canals were constructed, some by engineer Thomas Telford (1757-1834), to provide transport from the Midlands to nearby ports and other parts of England, for raw materials and manufactured goods.

Nonconformism had already begun to fester after the Act of Uniformity in 1662 which compelled clergy to conform closely to the Prayer Book. This outraged certain Presbyterian ministers in the Black Country and they left their churches. Consequently, unrest amongst the workers continued for some decades afterwards. After a service at Wednesbury (c38) a small group of Methodists started to meet together in the house of John Adams. Soon after the visit by Charles Wesley, the leader of the local Methodist society – Francis Ward – requested that his brother John should come to the town. This he did, arriving on 8 January 1743 preaching to coalminers from Wednesbury, nearby Walsall, and Darlaston (c38). A Methodist society of over one hundred had already been formed from the earlier visit by Charles. Later that year, John preached again in Wednesbury at an evening meeting in the Town Hall. On the following day, he preached in the town at five in the morning and, three hours later, in the Hollow – a natural amphitheatre (notorious for its bull-baiting and cock fights) about a mile from Wednesbury. That afternoon John went along to the parish church of St Bartholomew where he heard the vicar, the Reverend Edward Eggington, preach a 'plain but useful sermon'. Afterwards, John was invited back to Eggington's home where he was told he would always be made welcome in the town.

Wesley stated his aim was to preach to those people who did not have a church and emphasised that Methodist meetings were so arranged that they did not conflict with Anglican services. John preached again in the Hollow and three times in Wednesbury on the following day – with the result that membership of the society increased.

The situation was very different on his next visit on 15 April 1743. On that Sunday he returned to the parish church to hear Eggington preach. Wesley was dismayed to hear the vicar's derogatory comments against Methodists and described them as 'a wicked sermon and delivered with such bitterness of voice and manner'. As a result of this difference of opinion, Eggington and a group of furious Anglican colliers tried to destroy the Methodist society. In addition, John and his followers were very unpopular with those who organised blood sports or owned public houses as regular customers deserted them to attend prayer meetings. Yet despite the growing intimidation, Charles Wesley states that by May 1743 the society at Wednesbury had grown to three hundred. Matters were soon to come to a head.

John returned to Wednesbury on 20 October and preached from a horseblock on an open space called High Bullen situated in front of the parish church, a place he was afterwards to preach at on nearly forty occasions. (The mounting steps originally led to a malt house and the site is marked on Church Hill by a commemorative stone and plaque. The horseblock was later dismantled and removed to nearby Wednesbury Central Methodist Church in Spring Head where it can be seen together with the Dingley Collection of books and artefacts connected with the Wednesbury Riots of 1743-44).

Afterwards, John Wesley was taken to the home of Francis

*Horseblock from which Wesley preached*

Ward to conduct a prayer meeting (the house was originally at No. 92 Bridge Street – the site now occupied by Woden House). To their consternation, a mob surrounded Ward's house. Members of the society prayed it would soon disperse but Wesley was grabbed and manhandled by the crowd. They marched him off to Bentley Hall, a Carolean manor house, now demolished, to the east of Willenhall where they hoped the local magistrate, Mr JP Lane, might be on hand to charge him. (A cairn marks the site of Bentley Hall, the seat of the Lane family from the 15th to 18th centuries. The hall had earlier been visited on 9 September 1651 by Charles II, disguised as a groom, on his flight to freedom after the Battle of Worcester during the Civil War. Access to the cairn is from Cairn Drive, Bentley, quite close to the A454).

Mr Lane, the magistrate, refused to hear the case against Wesley and instructed them to go elsewhere. On their return to Wednesbury, fighting broke out between rival factions of the mob from Walsall and Darlaston, and a woman was dragged into the fracas and injured. A well-known prize-fighter and rough coal miner, George Clifton – better known as 'Honest Munchin' – managed to rescue the lady. The mob then decided to drag Wesley towards Walsall in their quest to find another magistrate, William Persehouse JP, of Reynolds Hall, and on this occasion were successful. However, all he could say to them was 'What do I want with Wesley?' and dismissed the case. (A section of Walsall Arboretum now occupies part of the grounds of the former Reynolds Hall on The Broadway, A4148).

In Walsall, Wesley received rough treatment from the crowd, and was thrown down the churchyard steps of St Matthew's Parish Church. This behaviour seems to have made a marked impressed on some of his attackers – including 'Honest Munchin' who was later credited with saving John's life. He began to protect the preacher and carried him across a stream to the safety of the opposite bank (the riverlet is now covered over by the area known as Digbeth). Eventually, Wesley was returned to the safety of the house of Francis Ward back in Wednesbury.

The following February, the properties and homes of local Methodists were systematically attacked during what were known as the 'Shrovetide Riots' which also involved mobs from other areas. Homes were broken into, goods and possessions seized, and individuals were injured and abused. Sometimes these mobs were encouraged by clergy of the Church of England in an effort to quell the growing tide of Methodism. Rioting in the area continued against Wesley for about six days but the persecution of Methodists lasted for about nine months. It was not a happy state of affairs.

Methodists in nearby West Bromwich also suffered persecution from the mob. John addressed a crowd in a preaching house in Paradise Street and also preached on two occasions in the courtyard of the Oak House (the building is a lovely black and white half-timbered yeoman's house of the 16th century with much character, and now an interesting museum. A plaque on an adjacent wall in the courtyard states that John Wesley preached there in 1774. Another Wesley memorial in the town was placed at the western end of the High Street precinct in 1988).

## Bishop Francis Asbury

It is perhaps pertinent at this stage to mention that it was from the West Bromwich area that Francis Asbury originated. He was to become the founding father of the American Methodist Church and was born on 21 August 1745 at nearby Hamstead. His parents moved to the hamlet of Newton at Great Barr when he was a few months old and young Francis spent his boyhood and early manhood in a cottage on Newton Road now known as Bishop Asbury's Cottage. It is just beyond the Malt Shovel Inn and stands apart from other housing. It once formed part of a row of cottages, the others having been demolished to allow road-widening some years ago.

Francis went to school at Snail's Green – about a mile away – but left at the age of twelve to become an apprentice to a local chape-maker, John Griffin (a chape was a buckle or metal plate at the end of a scabbard to protect the point of a sword). The Sandwell Valley area where the Asburys lived was owned by the 2nd Earl of Dartmouth, a Methodist supporter who was also a relation of George Washington. The Dartmouth estate included Sandwell Hall and its home farm, now the splendidly restored Sandwell Park Farm. Asbury's period of apprenticeship involved much manual work which built up his strength and stamina, both of which served him well in later years as a circuit rider.

The Asbury family attended worship at the parish churches of St Margaret's at Great Barr and All Saints at West Bromwich where the vicar was the Reverend Edward Stillingfleet, a man of Methodist enthusiasm and a friend of John Wesley.

At the age of eighteen young Francis attended a Methodist service at a chapel in Lloyd Street, Wednesbury, where he was converted. He soon became a lay preacher and delivered his first sermon at Manwoods Cottage in the Sandwell Valley. In 1766 Asbury left his work as a chape-maker to become a full time itinerant preacher and worked in Methodist circuits in Staffordshire, Bedfordshire, Gloucestershire and his final circuit – Wiltshire, where he was mainly based at Salisbury (a display of water colours depicting scenes from Asbury's life can be viewed in the present Salisbury Methodist church).

In August 1771 Francis attended his first Methodist conference at John Wesley's Chapel (the New Room) in Bristol, at the age of 26. It was here he heard Wesley appeal for preachers to go to America to spread the Word of God. Asbury volunteered and returned to Great Barr to inform his parents of his decision. He was never to see them again and on 4 September 1771 set sail from the little port of Pill on the River Avon near Bristol, bound for the New World and a new life. On reaching America, he arrived at Philadelphia and preached at St George's Church on the following day, 13 November 1771. Unlike earlier preachers who ventured across the Atlantic, Asbury adopted a policy of travelling the eastern side of America not only to cities and towns but also into the wilds of the mountains and rural areas.

During the American War of Independence, John Wesley ordered his Methodist preachers to return to England but Asbury refused. When the American Declaration of Independence was signed in July 1776 he stayed on to build up the American Methodist Church and, on Wesley's instructions, was ordained as its first pioneering Bishop on 24 December 1784 by Dr Thomas Coke, one of John Wesley's leading assistants. The ceremony took place at the Lovely Lane Chapel in Baltimore, built 1774, where a new denomination was born: the Methodist Episcopal Church in America. (Dr Coke had earlier been ordained by Wesley as 'superintendent' of the Methodist society in America.) In 1786, the chapel was relocated to nearby Light Street, and the original site on Lovely Lane (now Redwood Street) was later occupied by the Merchants Club, whose building now houses the Baltimore International College.

Bishop Francis Asbury died at Spottsylvania, Virginia, on 31 March 1816 but is now buried in Mount Olivet Cemetery in Baltimore. During his time in America it is estimated that he ordained over 3,000 preachers and preached over 17,000 sermons and, today, at least 600 churches in America are named Asbury Methodist Church after their founding father who was born in the Black Country. The Methodist Church in the USA now has a membership of some fifteen million people.

\* \* \*

Shortly after the riots in the Wednesbury area, Charles Wesley paid another visit to the town and discovered that 'Honest Munchin' had become a leader of the local Methodist society. He resided at a cottage, since demolished, at Hollow Bank and lived to be ninety. As the years went by, Wednesbury and other townships of the Black Country became established as some of the strongest bases of Methodism. The first Wesleyan preaching house in Darlaston was built in 1761 but the town's main Wesleyan chapel was built in Pinfold Street in 1810 and demolished a few years ago. At Bradley Methodist Chapel near Bilston is an iron pulpit from which John Wesley once preached.

In earlier years both John and Charles had encountered similar hostility in other parts of the Black Country. On a visit to Dudley (C39) on 24 October 1749, John writes in his Journal, 'At one, I went into the market place and proclaimed the name of the Lord to a huge, unwieldy, noisy multitude. I continued speaking for half an hour till some of Satan's servants pressed in raging and blaspheming and throwing whatever came to hand. I then retired to the house from which I came. The multitude poured after me and covered over with dirt many that were near me.' By 23 March 1764, he writes 'I rode to Dudley, formerly a den of lions, but now as quiet as Bristol.' (The area surrounding Dudley Castle where Wesley once preached is, ironically, now the site of Dudley Zoo.)

John Wesley visited Cradley in 1770 on a stormy windy day. A local folk rhyme goes:

> John Wesley had a bony hoss [bonny horse]
> The leanest e'er you sin. [ever you've seen]
> They took him down to Haysich brook
> And shoved him yedfast in! [headfirst in!]

This was not, in fact, true and seems to have become confused with a similar incident which took place on the bridge at Walsall in 1743.

Of a visit to Stourbridge on 19 March 1770, he also writes, 'About one I took the field at Stourbridge. Many of the hearers were wild as colts untamed; but the bridle was in their mouths'. Bilbrook was another place he called at to preach on 21 July 1764 whilst travelling to see his friend John Fletcher at Madeley (c36) in Shropshire.

John Wesley's first visit to Wolverhampton (c37) was not until March 1760 shortly after the first society had been formed by John Bennet and it appears he got quite a good reception. In the following year, he decided it was time he should preach in the open air to test public reaction. He subsequently arranged for a table to be placed in the yard of the Swan Inn at the top of the market place, now Queen Square. He said afterwards 'Such a number of wild men I have seldom seen but they gave me no disturbance'. Within twelve months of his sermon the first preaching house was built on the south side of Rotten Row (now Broad Street). It was destroyed by a mob in 1763 at the instigation of a lawyer named Hayes. Alexander Mather, the Methodist preacher, with the support of the 2nd Earl of Dartmouth, took legal action, which resulted in Hayes being ordered to rebuild the chapel at his own expense.

Two years later, the chapel proved too small and Wesley preached on 21 March 1770 outside the Angel Inn in a place called High Green below the market place. In the crowd was a young locksmith named Moseley, who threw a stone at John and hit him on the face causing blood to stream down his cheek. Wesley later converted him and he became a life-long Methodist and local preacher. Such incidents were not unusual for either of the Wesley brothers.

The local Methodist society in Wolverhampton soon outgrew its original home and on 28 March 1787, John opened a new chapel (called 'Noah's Ark' Chapel) in Wheeler's Fold, so named because it stood in the yard of a pub with that title in Lichfield

Street, opposite St Peter's Gardens. He made two further visits to the town in 1788 and 1790, the latter being when he addressed 'a numerous and respectable audience'. John Wesley died the following year. By 1815 the chapel in Wheeler's Fold had become too small and the congregation moved to a new site in Darlington Street which has been in continuous use and has remained the town's centre for Methodism to the present day. (A wall frieze has been erected in the modern Wulfrun shopping centre depicting Wesley's preaching in the town.)

Wesley also preached at other Black Country chapels or sites – in Temple Street, Bilston, as early as 1743; Cotterell's Farm, Toll End in Tipton; Bullocks Fold in Bloxwich; and in 1781 at Quinton. Many Methodist chapels and churches sprang up across the conurbation, too numerous to mention, but a perfectly-preserved Methodist chapel can be visited at the excellent Black Country Living Museum (C39) on Tipton Road in Dudley. This building, a former chapel of the Methodist New Connexion, was originally built in 1837 at Darby Hand, Netherton. It was dismantled and re-erected on the museum site in 1977 and completed two years later. The Museum is one of the finest open air sites in Britain. A range of buildings has been re-erected from all over the area to form a typical Black Country community, peopled by costumed guides and interpreters to explain the hardships of life during the Industrial Revolution and afterwards. The foundations of Methodism as first laid down by John and Wesley and their fellow preachers are still very much in evidence across the Black Country today.

# CHAPTER 9

# Staffordshire, Shropshire, Peak District, Cheshire

PRIOR TO BOUNDARY changes in 1974 much of the Black Country was part of Staffordshire until it was absorbed into the new county of West Midlands. We therefore trace John Wesley's steps into other parts of Staffordshire and the adjacent counties of Shropshire, Derbyshire and Cheshire, regular places of call during his travels across the country.

North of Wolverhampton and close to the M54 motorway (Junction 1) is a palatial mansion set in its own estate called Hilton Park Hall, which was formerly the home of the Vernon family. Henry Vernon built the hall in the early 18th century, close to the site of an original manor house, with the main front facing a lake. It was here on 28 March 1785 that John Wesley was a guest of Sir Philip Gibbes, whose family were supporters of the growing Methodist movement. John is known to have written a number of letters to, and visited, Mary and Agnes Gibbes both of whom he had known since childhood. The house ceased to be family-owned in the 1950s when it became a Roman Catholic rest home and, later, was sold for commercial use as headquarters of a major construction company.

In total, Wesley paid six visits to the town of Stafford, though in 1738 and 1746 he was merely passing through on his way to the Potteries area. His next visit was in 1783 when Methodists were using a converted stable as their place of worship. On this occasion John found very little notification of his coming had taken place – with the result that only a few people turned up to hear him. He was there again twice in the next two years, the second occasion in 1785 being more joyous as he opened the new preaching house, built at the corner of Cherry Street and Broad Eye. John comments in his Journal on 29 March – 'At noon I preached in the room at Stafford to a deeply affected congregation. This was strange, because there are few towns in England less infected with religion.' This chapel was used for worship for thirteen years but, due to dwindling interest and support, was sold by auction and turned into a cottage. As Wesleyan Methodism began to grow in Stafford a new chapel was built on Earl Street in 1812, of which a tower still remains.

The fast M54 motorway leads to the new town of Telford and on towards Shrewsbury. However, we need to leave this highway and follow signs for Ironbridge and Madeley (C36), an important centre of early Methodism. By the time of Wesley's visits, Nonconformism – especially Quakerism – had also been established in this area of the East Shropshire coalfield.

Ironbridge, now a World Heritage Site, was an early birthplace of the Industrial Revolution and takes it name from the massive first iron bridge over the River Severn. On a visit to the area in 1779, John Wesley admired the bridge prior to it being hauled and erected into position. The fast-flowing river cuts through the heavily wooded limestone gorge, populated on the northern bank by a small township of narrow, steep-winding streets and alleyways (the late international footballer and former 'Wolves' player, Billy Wright, spent his boyhood here). Leading off in a northerly direction is Coalbrookdale where, in 1709, a Quaker ironmaster, Abraham Darby, pioneered the use of coke in iron smelting instead of scarcer and more expensive charcoal. His works were to revolutionise the whole iron industry. It was here that coal, with local iron ore and limestone, cradled the Industrial Revolution. The many natural resources of the area led to other industries being set up in the district, such as the china works at Caughley and Coalport, and later, the Tile Works at Jackfield. Today, it is difficult to believe the area was a thriving industrial centre during the 18th and 19th centuries. Instead, the visitor will find a tranquil environment of great natural beauty. There are a number of important industrial monuments which form the core

*Ironbridge, Shropshire*

of the award-winning Ironbridge Gorge Museum. There are six museums to visit and other sites of interest or information points.

A mile or so from the Ironbridge Gorge is the township of Madeley which Wesley occasionally visited to stay with his close friend, Reverend John Fletcher who was vicar between 1760-85.

## John Fletcher

John Fletcher was born Jean Guillaume de la Fléchère at Nyon on the northern shore of Lake Geneva on 12 September 1729 and originally intended to take up military service abroad. Instead, he came to England in 1752 where he became a tutor to Thomas Hill's family at Tern Hall, Atcham, Shropshire. The house was rebuilt by his son Noel and is today known as Attingham Park (National Trust) and open to the public. Hill was one of two MPs for the town of Shrewsbury. Whilst in England Fletcher met John and Charles Wesley and was later ordained a deacon, then priest, in the Church of England on 6 March 1757. He preached his first sermon in Atcham parish church. Just over three years later he was inaugurated as vicar of Madeley where he soon came to terms with his parishioners and new surroundings.

John Fletcher instituted religious society meetings in Madeley Wood and nearby Coalbrookdale which were regularly visited by itinerant preachers such as Wesley, Whitefield and their followers. John Wesley's first visit was on 21 July 1764 when he stayed for two days and, later, paid seven further visits to the area during Fletcher's ministry. During the 1760s Fletcher extended his work into a much wider area of the Shropshire coalfield and also became Superintendent of Trefeca College (E30) in South Wales from which he later resigned after some disagreement. Nevertheless, his reputation for evangelical work increased nationally along with his literary talents and in 1772 he produced an important theological work, *An Appeal to Matter of Fact and Common Sense*. He was 52 when, in 1781, he married Mary Bosanquet, a prominent Methodist woman preacher, whom he had known for some time. Mary was to prove invaluable in helping with his ministry. Increasingly, Wesley felt that Fletcher was the man to take over from him as leader of the Methodist movement at his own death. It was not be as John Fletcher died six years before Wesley. Mary Fletcher continued her husband's work and ministry in the area for another thirty years.

The visitor to Madeley can see Fletcher sites such as the iron box grave of John and Mary to the left of the main entrance to the present parish church (the original building had to be demolished). This church was designed by the great engineer Thomas Telford and opened for public worship in 1797. The Old Vicarage, once Fletcher's home, is a five-bay brick building to the north-east of the church but with a much altered interior. It is now a guest house, where visitors can sleep in the Fletcher rooms. The site of the Vicarage Barn where Mary Fletcher held meetings once stood between the Old Vicarage and the corner of Station Road. The place where she stood to preach is still visible. Proceeding towards Madeley town centre from the corner of Station Road along Church Street one finds, on the right beyond Church Close, a former infants school which is now a private residence. This was the first Wesleyan chapel in the town centre and opened on 14 August 1833. Beyond the end of Church Road stands the Fletcher Methodist Church, opened in 1841.

\* \* \*

ON THE TRAIL OF JOHN WESLEY

Higher up the Severn is the medieval town of Shrewsbury (C35) – the central part of which sits neatly in a large meander of the river, making it almost an island. It is the setting for the Brother Cadfael series of books by Shropshire author Ellis Peters who set most of the novels in Shrewsbury Abbey. It was also a place which John Wesley knew well, and the small white double-fronted cottage, No.1 Fish Street, where he preached on his first visit on Thursday 16 March 1761 is still marked by a plaque. It stands opposite the now redundant church of St Alkmund's and the thoroughfare leads up to Butcher Row, Grope Lane and a series of half-timbered black and white buildings. John often stayed in the road known as Dog Pole with Mrs. Bridget Glynne, an hospitable and quite well-to-do Methodist lady. The road still boasts a number of fine 18th century town houses.

The influence of both John Wesley and John Fletcher on Shropshire was great and is evidenced by the number of Methodist churches and chapels spread around the county. There are still many thriving Nonconformist communities in these areas.

Much of the county boundary in North Shropshire runs alongside part of North West Staffordshire, another coal-mining area generally known as the Potteries (C28). It was originally made up of six separate towns which amalgamated to become the city of Stoke-on-Trent in 1910. The area also gained recognition through the novels of Burslem-born author Arnold Bennett who used it as a background setting for novels such as *Clayhanger, Anna of the Five Towns*, and *The Card*. It was also the birthplace of another famous international footballer, Sir Stanley Matthews, and pop singer, Robbie Williams. The Potteries found itself at the forefront of the Industrial Revolution, thanks to great figures like Josiah Wedgwood and canal builder James Brindley, and the presence of mineral deposits of coal and clay necessary for the pottery industry. It was at Burslem that Gilbert Wedgwood is recorded as the first Master Potter of his family in 1640. Some of the potteries are open to visitors including Wedgwood, Royal Doulton and Spode.

Around 300 years ago a track known as the Lane ran from

Tunstall to Longton, linking a string of villages along an eight-mile (12.9 km) route including Burslem, Hanley, Stoke, Fenton and Lane End (later Longton). Although these places were each developing the pottery industry, they were still much influenced by nearby Newcastle-under-Lyme, an ancient market town. It is little wonder that John Wesley saw the growing area as a place for ministry and included it in his travels.

Wesley first preached in Newcastle-under-Lyme as early as 1738, the year of his conversion. However, his first visit to Stoke-on-Trent was on 8 March 1760 when he spoke at a large meeting in Burslem. He often visited the town where the first Methodist society in the county was formed at Swan Bank Methodist Church after earlier visits to meetings in Bristol by Potteries coal miners. On 28 March 1781, Wesley comments in his Journal about the great changes which had taken place over the twenty years since his first visit. This was undoubtedly caused by rapid industrial expansion with people flocking in from rural areas. In Newcastle-under-Lyme Wesley preached in the market place to a large crowd and stayed overnight at the mayor's home. He described the town as 'one of the prettiest in England'. In 1784 at Longton, the meeting room he had been designated would not hold a quarter of the people who wanted to attend so Wesley preached outside in the moonlight. In the same year he also paid his first visit to Hanley. He was to continue to travel to the Potteries area over a thirty year period. 'Sinners are daily awakened and converted to God,' he wrote. It was on Sunday 28 March 1790 that John preached one of his last sermons in the yard of the Old Foley Pottery in Fenton. On this visit he also preached at the new chapel at Tunstall – the Wesley Place Methodist Church which was later converted into an old people's home.

## Primitive Methodism –
## Hugh Bourne and William Clowes

It was in 1749 that John Wesley first visited that area of

Staffordshire which borders onto Cheshire and which was soon to become a place of significant development in the Methodist Church. From the early work of John and his lay preachers, a number of small groups had been formed as part of the growing Methodist movement. It was here that Primitive Methodism first took its roots.

In 1807 a large open air meeting was held at a local Staffordshire beauty spot known as Mow Cop (c27), the aim being to pray and bring the Gospel to people outside of church life. In the main this was the work of two men – Hugh Bourne and William Clowes. Bourne was born on 3 April 1772 at Ford Hayes Farm, Hayes Lane, Stoke-on-Trent, his father being a bluff temperamental man. His mother was a loving and moral influence on Hugh and his brother. When Hugh was sixteen, the Bourne family moved to Bemersley Farm near Tunstall. After some years of personal struggle with his conscience, he was converted at the age of 27 and joined the Methodist Church. Before long he was organising prayer groups and large outdoor meetings for worship, known as Camp Meetings. Wesleyan Methodists began to disapprove of his radical activities, based partly on American influences, and expelled him in 1808. (Bemersley Farm and Barn were later used as the Primitive Methodist printing works and book room. The printing staff included Hugh Bourne, his brother James and others.)

William Clowes was born in Burslem in 1780, son of an ungodly potter, but with a kindly mother. At the age of ten, he became an apprentice potter who soon developed a taste for dancing, frivolity and drunkenness. During an incident in Hull in 1803, he narrowly escaped being press-ganged into the Marines, and returned to Tunstall leaving a trail of debts behind him. Two years later he attended a service and prayer meeting where he felt the hand of God upon him. As a result, he cleared his debts and joined the Methodist society at Tunstall, and soon began preaching the Gospel. It was not long before he met Hugh Bourne, a man of similar persuasion, and joined him in organising his Camp Meetings. As with Bourne, Clowes was also condemned by the Wesleyan Methodists for his passionate style of Methodism, and left their company.

Mow Cop is a rocky outcrop in an elevated position offering wide vistas over surrounding countryside and surmounted by a mid-18th century folly known as Mow Cop Castle, built for Randle Wilbraham who lived at nearby Rode Hall. A stone has been erected to commemorate the first Camp Meeting. The actual site is off Woodcock Lane close to the Memorial Chapel erected in 1852 (C27) and now a local history museum. Noisy cottage prayer meetings and loud singing in the streets of the Potteries became a regular feature of these new and enthusiastic Revivalists and they were soon nicknamed the 'Ranters' and, later, became known as 'Primitive Methodists.'

In many ways this was the re-discovery of New Testament Christianity and William Clowes independently travelled the country as an itinerant preacher to spread his message. Hugh Bourne became another revered leader and lived a life of great simplicity and sacrifice. He did not allow a foot ailment to prevent him walking miles to preach, despite the swelling. He died in 1852 and his body was brought from Bemersley Farm to lie in Engelsea Brook Primitive Methodist chapel prior to burial, at his own request, in the chapel graveyard. By the time of his death, Primitive Methodism had 100,000 members. Clowes' health also deteriorated as he continued with the rigours of itinerant preaching and retired to Hull to continue his work. He died in 1851 and was buried in Hull General Cemetery. Though very different personalities, the combined talents of the two men did much to establish this new form of Methodism.

The oldest Primitive Methodist chapel still in use is at Cloud Side, Rushton, near Congleton, which was erected in 1815. It offers splendid views across to the foothills of the Pennines. The Chapel at Engelsea Brook has become an excellent flagship Museum of Primitive Methodism (C29) and stems from Clowes' side of the movement. It is situated in a pretty hamlet just over three miles from Junction 16 of the M6 motorway (follow the A500 – signposted Crewe – and B5078) and is recorded as a place of preaching in 1811. A schoolroom extension in memory of Hugh Bourne was added in 1914. As well as many Sunday School banners, trophies, photographs and portraits, a feature of the museum is that parties of schoolchildren are given a typical Victorian style Sunday School, complete with schoolmistress and costumes. In those days, Primitive Methodist Sunday School lessons also included the times-tables and sums. Singing is still sometimes accompanied by the 1828 pipe organ, and an audio visual and 'magic lantern' presentation both provide a vivid glimpse into the past.

\* \* \*

The Roman city of Chester (C30) was a regular calling place of John Wesley en route for Ireland and it became the Methodist centre for quite a large area which encompassed parts of Shropshire, Manchester and some of the new industrial towns of Lancashire. On his first visit he preached near St John's Church in Chester after an open air meeting and, later, regularly addressed the crowds in an area known as the Roodee, now Chester racecourse. He would have been very familiar with the red sandstone walls and towers of the city along with the magnificent Chester Cathedral, once an 11th century Benedictine abbey, and the famous Rows with their covered galleries. A figure of John Wesley in stained glass can be seen in the cloisters of the Cathedral. After his first visit, a mob attacked the preaching house and completely destroyed it. On his next visit, undaunted, he preached near the shell of the old building and afterwards attended a service at St Martin's Church. On a temporary basis, his Chester congregation re-commenced their meetings in Love Lane and eventually rebuilt their preaching house in the Square.

Macclesfield, once famous for its silk mills, is another Cheshire town where Wesley preached on many occasions, often in an area known as Water's Green, a fine open square below the parish church. Christ Church was built in 1775 both for Wesley's preaching and the evangelical ministry of the Reverend David

Simpson, curate of the parish church and a friend of Wesley. Simpson was also a pioneer of Sunday schools and the church had spacious galleries with a high pulpit and organ which once belonged to Handel. Today, the building is owned by the Churches' Conservation Trust and is open to the public on certain dates. The town centre congregation first started to meet in a stable beyond Temple Bar and then rented a small preaching house. A local benefactor, John Ryle, provided land and material for a new Wesley's Chapel in Sunderland Street.

Wesley would have crossed the hills to reach New Mills and other villages in the Peak District. On 24 May 1783 he arrived by chaise from Derby and preached in the spa town of Buxton, also conducting the wedding of two of his followers in St Anne's Church. He delivered his message in many Peakland villages and towns such as Hayfield (where he stayed at the Royal Hotel), Leek and Chapel-en-le-Frith. John was caught out in a snowstorm on 23 March 1765 on his way from Bradwell to preach at Eyam woodlands and took shelter at the remote wind-swept Barrel Inn at Bretton Clough. He also travelled the same route twelve months later. Crich near Matlock has one of the oldest Methodist chapels in the Peak District, dating from 1765 (this small town is close to the site of the National Tramway Museum). In the nearby lushly-wooded valley of the River Derwent lies Cromford, another early site of the Industrial Revolution which was enjoying its heyday during the time of John Wesley. It was here that Sir William Arkwright set up the first water-powered cotton spinning mill which has since, rather like the Ironbridge Gorge, been named as a World Heritage Site. Willersley Castle, once Arkwright's splendid mansion overlooking the river valley, has become an attractive Methodist holiday home. On 27 July 1761 John Wesley preached under the hollow of a rock in nearby Matlock Bath, once a spa town like its near neighbour of Matlock. The limestone rock scenery of the precipitous High Tor is outstanding as it towers over the river valley far below.

Travelling northwards along the valley of the River Derwent is Chatsworth, the magnificent home of the Duke and Duchess of

Devonshire, and the charming villages of Baslow and Calver – Cliff College (c20), a famous Methodist institution dedicated to training people in evangelistic ministry, is situated in the latter. The area forms the southern part of the Pennines and contains much wild, open, heather-clad moorland and mountainous terrain. Wesley pursued his journeying whatever the weather or difficulties along the way. One of the remotest places in which he once sheltered was a barn at Alport Castles Farm reached along Alport Dale (access only on foot) – reached from the A57 Snake Pass road and following the river towards Bleaklow Hill. An annual Love Feast ceremony, when hymns are sung and the congregation partake of plum loaf and water, still takes place in the building on the first Sunday in July.

On that occasion, Wesley was travelling from Lancashire to Yorkshire – a place which still has many associated sites for those who wish to follow in his footsteps.

# CHAPTER 10

# Lincolnshire and Yorkshire

QUITE A FEW YEARS had passed by the time John Wesley returned to his birthplace at Epworth on Saturday 5 June 1742. It was to prove a rather traumatic visit. After staying at the Red Lion Inn, the local hostelry, he offered his assistance to the local curate to help or preach at the Sunday morning service in St Andrew's Parish Church. His offer was refused. In consequence, John preached outside the church at six in the evening whilst standing on his own father's tombstone, where a vast crowd turned out to hear him. He was to visit Epworth again on numerous occasions – sometimes on his way to Grimsby or to reach the Hull ferry across the River Humber.

South of Epworth on the River Trent is the town of Gainsborough (C23) with its magnificent Old Hall, a half-timbered building erected about 1460 by Sir Thomas Burgh. It is a former manor house which stands in Lord Street, having a stone tower with oriel window, towers of small bricks and the whole forming three sides of a quadrangle. It is one of the largest and best-preserved medieval buildings in England, and is open to the public. The building has many historic associations including visits by Richard III, Henry VIII and his sixth wife, Catherine Parr, and some of the early Separatists led by John Smyth. John Wesley preached in the magnificent great hall on at least two occasions as the owner, Sir Neville Hickman, had Nonconformist leanings. A special display on the Methodist connection can be viewed in the building.

Mention must be made of the county town of Lincoln (C24) with its magnificent Gothic cathedral which Wesley much admired and thought even more elegant than York Minster. He preached in the yard of nearby Lincoln Castle, which also housed the county jail. In the nearby hall the Shire Court was held. The castle also possesses one of four surviving copies of the Magna Carta signed by King John in 1215. Of particular historic interest is the prison chapel where prisoners were allowed to attend services. Each convict was segregated into an individual high box pew from where they could see the preacher but not one another – yet the preacher could see every one of them!

When John first went to Boston (F1) in 1759 he found Methodism already established in the port. Two years previously, Alexander Mather, (referred to later in this chapter) one of Wesley's converts and preachers, had gone there and founded the first society in the area. Wesley paid further visits in 1761 and 1780 when, at the age of 77, he climbed to the top of St Botolph's Parish Church, the tallest church tower in England and known affectionately as 'Boston Stump'. It says much for his physical condition, despite the hardships of travel faced during his life. From the top of the church tower he would, no doubt, have marvelled at the extensive views across the flatlands of Lincolnshire and to the open sea. A painting of John preaching from his father's tomb at Epworth can be seen at Boston Guildhall in South Street, a building where some of the original Pilgrim Fathers had earlier been imprisoned in 1607, after their first abortive attempt to escape to Holland in search of religious freedom.

The oldest Methodist chapel in Lincolnshire and, indeed, one of the oldest in the country is at Raithby-by-Spilsby (C26). It was opened by John Wesley in July 1779 and built over a stable. The interior of the chapel is Georgian and has been well preserved. It is unique in that it is not owned by the Methodist Church but belongs to the owners of the private Raithby Hall, the house built by the founder of the chapel, Robert Carr Brackenbury (1752-1818), one of Wesley's preachers. Brackenbury was a close friend of Wesley and had earlier worked in the Isle of Portland and the Channel Isles. Undoubtedly, on his visits to Raithby, John would have stabled his horse in the area beneath the Methodist chapel. On a later visit to preach in July 1788, he records 'We went to

Raithby: an earthly paradise! How gladly would I rest here a few days; but it is not my place! I am to be a wanderer upon earth. Only let me find rest in a better world!' Visitors to Raithby Chapel should note that only foot access is allowed across the private stable yard.

Wesley occasionally called at Grantham (F2) when he was travelling along the Great North road. His first visit was in 1747 when he stayed at the White Lion Inn. He later preached in the open air behind the house of Thomas Derry in Watergate.

\* \* \*

Crossing into the southern tip of South Yorkshire is the city of Sheffield (C21), set in a large hollow and, rather like Rome, surrounded by seven hills divided by river valleys which provided water power to drive early industrial machinery. The charcoal and iron ore content of the local Hallamshire hills provided the necessary raw materials for the growth of the city's cutlery and steel industries. Sheffield was another place where a rural population had flocked to seek new employment in the 18th century and, in total, Wesley visited the town on forty occasions. He first preached there in June 1742, followed by his brother Charles the following year. John's final visit was in July 1788 at the age of 85.

Undoubtedly, the most historic occasion was on 15 July 1779 when John Wesley preached in the lovely Georgian Paradise Square from the first floor doorway of No.18, once reached by a stone staircase. He records in his Journal that he addressed 'the largest congregation I ever saw on a weekday.' The square today is still full of atmosphere and has a real sense of history. Buildings include town houses from Georgian and Victorian periods and are excellent examples of how the Anglo-Palladian style had been adapted to meet the aspirations of the new middle classes. No. 24 was once occupied by a portrait painter, Francis Chantrey, who was knighted after he became the best known British sculptor of the late 18th and early 19th centuries. He is buried at the lovely

Norman parish church of St James in the suburb of Norton where he was born.

Up the hill from Paradise Square is Sheffield Cathedral, the former parish church, where Wesley preached in July 1780 – there were afterwards 'such a number of communicants as was never seen at the old church before'. A desk used by Wesley can be viewed in the cathedral together with a stained glass window in the Chapter House which depicts his preaching in Paradise Square. (A statue of the famous hymn writer, poet and former editor of the Sheffield Iris, James Montgomery, is sited at the eastern end of the cathedral yard close to East Parade. Amongst many others, he wrote the hymn *Angels from the Realms of Glory*.) From here it is only a short walk to the Victoria Methodist Mission on Norfolk Street which has an interesting display of Wesleyana. The church is built on the site of the former Norfolk Street Chapel where Wesley preached at the official opening in 1780.

North of Sheffield is a small hamlet called Barley Hall near Thorpe Hesley, where John preached on numerous occasions and stayed overnight at Barley Hall Farm (usually after preaching in Doncaster, Rotherham and in the market place at Barnsley). A horse block on the village green in Thorpe Hesley commemorates

*Paradise Square, Sheffield*

the links. A mile or so away is the former stately home of Wentworth Woodhouse, former home of the Earls Fitzwilliam, which greatly impressed Wesley when he visited in July 1786 as it has the longest façade of any stately home in England. He compared the Stables Block with Tom Quadrangle at Christ Church in Oxford. John also preached in nearby Wentworth at the 13th century parish church of the Holy Trinity.

\* \* \*

The River Calder flows eastwards from the Pennines and cuts through steep valleys and a string of towns once made famous by the cloth manufacturing industry with wool supplied by the Pennine sheep. It was a hive of activity in Wesley's day and a regular route on his travels. On top of the wild windswept moors and situated on a quiet road across the hills to Burnley sits Todmorden Edge Farm. It is special in Methodist history for being where the first Quarterly Meeting was held in 1748, the forerunner of every Circuit Meeting since. This meeting, first instituted by John Wesley, is held four times a year in the Methodist calendar and brings together ministers, preachers and officials of the various churches and chapels in each Methodist society to discuss matters of policy and administration. The Farm is privately owned but can be viewed from the exterior.

Only a few miles to the east is the unspoiled village of Heptonstall (C14), a stark medieval and Jacobean village built of local millstone grit, dramatically perched on the edge of a steep hillside. Dominating the scene is the square tower of the 19th century parish church and an earlier church, now ruined, originally built between 1256-60. It occupies the same churchyard as the Victorian replacement. It was in the older building that the rector invited Wesley to preach in April 1774. Around are former weavers' cottages, an old cloth hall, and the 17th century former grammar school – now a museum. A little lower down in the village is the famous Methodist octagonal chapel, built in 1764 and open daily to visitors. (The shape of the chapel is related to what is known as Wesley's 'octagonal period'. In 1757 he visited the splendid Octagonal Chapel built by the Presbyterian Dr Taylor in Norwich (F8). Although disapproving of its costly interior, Wesley was greatly taken by its shape and encouraged Methodist builders to follow suit. 'It is best for the voice' he wrote in his Journal. During the period 1761-1776, fourteen of these chapels were built. Only three remain today in Methodist use.) At Heptonstall, the local builder was unable to construct the roof, so it was made at Rotherham in the south of the county, carried across country and hauled up the hill by the villagers.

Whilst in Heptonstall it is worth taking a look at No. 4 Northgate. Known as the Preacher's House, it is the place where the local Methodist society first met, a double-fronted cottage which opens onto the street. A walk around Heptonstall gives the visitor the opportunity to see a typical Yorkshire community where time seems to have stood still. A few miles north is Haworth, world-famous as the home of the Brontë sisters of literary fame. They spent most of their lives at Haworth Parsonage, now a museum, where their father, the Reverend Patrick Brontë, was once Rector. Haworth is a similar village to Heptonstall and clings to the hillside with a steep cobbled street at its heart. On more than one occasion Wesley attracted such a large congregation in Haworth that he was forced to deliver his sermon in the churchyard of St Michael and All Angels. Heptonstall remains unspoilt while Haworth has become over-commercialised and overrun by thousands of visitors.

Wesley preached in various chapels and churches in what is now known as Calderdale, in places such as Todmorden, Sowerby Bridge, Mytholmroyd, Hebden Bridge, Elland and Halifax. Close to Halifax is Ogden Moor where the historic Mount Zion Chapel (C13) stands. It originated from a visit to Halifax by John Wesley on 22 August 1748. He preached in the town and among the crowd that day was a man named James Riley. He was obviously deeply impressed with the great preacher and is quoted as saying 'Wesley disturbed my conscience and troubled my soul'. The following Sunday Riley decided to travel to Haworth to listen to the Reverend William Grimshaw. This was to result in the formation of a house meeting in a cottage in Bradshaw Row, Halifax.

By 1773 the Methodists of north Halifax needed a chapel for worship and the outcome was the building of Mount Zion Chapel and the adjoining cottage, which were opened in 1773. The following April Wesley came to stay in the cottage and preach in the chapel. His last visit to Halifax was in May 1790 when he again preached at Mount Zion as a frail 87-year old.

## Methodist New Connection – Alexander Kilham

After Wesley's death there was growing dissent in the Methodist Church which resulted in some new breakaway groups, such as that led by Alexander Kilham. Kilham was also born in Epworth, in 1762 – much later than the Wesleys – and was the son of a weaver. He became a Methodist local preacher at the age of twenty and soon became one of John Wesley's travelling preachers. It was not long before he made a name for himself as a powerful writer and orator and soon began to press for greater lay representation in the way Wesleyan Methodism was governed.

His views angered fellow preachers and his proposals were turned down. He persisted with his stance and eventually, in 1796, was put on trial and expelled from membership of the Methodist Church by the Wesleyan Conference. As a result, he started the New Methodist Connexion a year later – a major branch of the Methodist Church. Alexander Kilham was appointed as its Secretary, but died shortly afterwards.

The group was very strong at Mount Zion, Halifax, and it was successful in evicting the Wesleyan Methodists to a nearby barn. Mount Zion is the oldest Methodist New Connexion society which has continuously met. The church was demolished (except for the preachers' quarters) and replaced by the present building in 1815. The interior of the chapel is traditional with gallery and pews of pitch pine and was completed in 1881. The fine organ was built in 1892 by Charles Anneessens and Son of Belgium. The building also houses the splendid Horace Hird Collection of Methodist Ceramics and is open on certain days.

\* \* \*

The town of Halifax is well-known for its Piece Hall, first opened in 1779, where worsted cloth was sold in 'pieces'. It is one of Europe's finest 18th century architectural buildings, at which John Wesley had marvelled in his own day. Today, the site is a browser's delight and the open square is the setting for many important events and gatherings. The open space is surrounded on four sides by buildings with colonnaded galleries, which house a multitude of arts and craft outlets, book and antique shops, and the Calderdale Industrial Museum.

Leaving Calderdale for the valley of the River Spen, we come to Gomersal near Cleckheaton, where the Red House, built in the classical style in 1660, is said to have been visited by John Wesley. The elegant Georgian Hall, so named because of its red brick construction, was later the home of the Taylor family who entertained Charlotte Brontë. She was obviously impressed with her stay as it provided the inspiration for the 'Yorkes' family and the house called 'Briarmains' in her novel *Shirley*. The building is now a interesting museum and is furnished as it might have been in the 1820s. It is open to the public and contains a mirror which once belonged to John Nelson, one of Wesley's lay preachers who was known as the pioneer of Methodism in Yorkshire.

## John Nelson

John Nelson's house is in nearby Birstall where he was born in 1707. A travelling stonemason whose work often took him to London, he heard Wesley preach at Moorfields in June 1739. Nelson felt Wesley was looking right at him and penetrating his thoughts. By the end of the year John Nelson had given his heart to the Lord and taken up preaching. He dreamt that Wesley came to visit him and this actually came true in May 1742 when the great preacher passed through Nelson's home town of Birstall on his journey to Newcastle.

From then on Nelson developed the Yorkshire Methodist societies and became one of Wesley's most faithful itinerant preachers and helpers. Nelson sometimes accompanied Wesley on his long journeys. His study still stands in the grounds of the former Birstall Methodist Church which he founded in 1750 on the Huddersfield road. It consists of a small single cell building, dated 1751, and was built by Nelson in brick with a slate roof and corner chimney. The structure also has a single doorway and two small side windows. At the time of his death, on 18 July 1774, John Nelson was still serving as a Methodist preacher in Leeds. It is reported that thousands of people lined the funeral route and many followed the cortege from there to Birstall where he was laid to rest in the graveyard of the parish church. A brass tablet was also erected in the church in his memory.

* * *

John Wesley often preached in Leeds (C12), which became a centre of Methodism. He was attacked by an unruly mob when he visited the town in 1745. It was, later, one of three places chosen by John to hold the Annual Conference – the others being London and Bristol. The first Conference to be held in Leeds, in May 1753, was particularly important as it was when the question of women preachers was discussed. John spoke in favour of the motion – with certain reservations – and the result was that some of the first lady preachers in Methodism became active in Leeds and surrounding areas. One of these was a local woman, Sarah Crosby (1729-1804). She was born in Leeds and, when younger, had been drawn to the Calvinist Church. She was attracted to Methodism on hearing Wesley preach. After her husband's desertion she moved to London in 1757 to work as a class leader at the Foundery. Four years later she moved to Derby and became one of the first female preachers in Methodism. Sarah eventually returned to Leeds and is buried in the graveyard of St Peter's Parish Church on Kirkgate. Two other women preachers are also interred there – Ann Tripp and Sarah Ryan – and a nearby plaque commemorates the work and lives of the three women.

St Peter's is the main Anglican church in Leeds and was an important site connected with the growth of the Nonconformist cause. The main Methodist centre was a place called Boggard House – the first Methodist chapel in Leeds – where Annual Conferences were held.

This unusual name came about as follows: the first indoor preaching house for Methodists was an empty property provided by William Shent, a barber and wig maker – one of the leaders of the local society. He became a lay preacher and, in 1742, invited John Nelson to preach outside his shop in what was then the market place. The site became a regular preaching point for others, including John and Charles Wesley, and the shop became the first Methodist base. As in other towns, the Methodists in Leeds had their share of mob violence and moved to several sites before receiving help from a basket maker named Matthew Chippendale. His house stood in a field called Applegarth – and a local name for this was Boggard Close (or 'field'). It served the Methodists until 1751, when a new chapel and premises were built around the old framework. It was later known as Old Boggard until replacement by St Peter's Chapel in 1834. All traces of the Old Boggard site have since been obliterated.

John Wesley was a regular visitor to other West Yorkshire towns such as Huddersfield, Dewsbury, Wakefield, Bradford, and smaller communities. On 29 April 1779 he preached at Rothwell and Leeds, then the following day at Harewood where he was taken to see Harewood House. The building was owned by the Lascelles family and was also the home of the late Princess Royal, Princess Mary, daughter of George V. Wesley describes it in his Journal as 'of fine white stone, with two grand and beautiful fronts'. However, he was not keen on anything he saw within the house.

John visited the county town of York (C10) on twenty-six occasions when he would see the towering Minster, medieval walls, ancient buildings, 'snickels' (alleyways) and historic streets such as the Shambles, Stonegate and Low Petergate. His first visit was on 25 April 1752 when the Methodists borrowed the Countess of Huntingdon's Chapel, which once stood in College Street. The small society moved to the ancient Chapel of St Sepulchre, also no longer extant, attached to the north-west tower of the Minster and known as the 'Hole in the Wall.' Later the society moved to a room in Pump Yard near the market (nicknamed 'the oven' due to its overheated atmosphere in summer and now commemorated by a plaque). Eventually, a site for a chapel was acquired in Aldwark, off Peaseholme Green. On 18 April 1759 Wesley preached in York's first Methodist chapel to a 'large congregation'. Though no longer used as a chapel, the building is marked by a plaque. It served the growing Methodist society until it was replaced by an octagonal chapel in New Street in 1805. On one visit Wesley was invited to preach in St Saviour's church and stayed at the nearby Black Swan Inn.

On the centenary of John Wesley's conversion of 24 May 1738, a decision was made to build a grander chapel to seat 1,500 people. As a result, the Methodist society built and opened in 1840 their new chapel on St Saviourgate, designed by James Simpson of Leeds – now known as York Central Methodist Church. It has an imposing classical façade incorporating a large three-bay portico of unfluted Ionic columns and pediment. The interior is equally elaborate and the church welcomes visitors on a regular basis.

A few miles east of York is the pretty market town of Beverley which also has an imposing minster though smaller than that at York. Wesley considered it 'a stately building both within and without and kept more nicely clean than any cathedral I have seen in the kingdom'. He preached there in the yard of the White Horse Inn in Hengate and in Hilton Yard. John slept in a small room at No. 47 North Bar Street Within. Beverley is a bustling little town with a thriving Saturday market which sells a wide variety of goods. It proves a magnet for visitors from a wide area.

Close by is the fishing port of Hull (c11) on the River Humber. Its quayside was full of spectators when John arrived to preach in

Holy Trinity Church and in a field near Great Thornton Street. He often travelled along the Yorkshire coast to speak to fisher-folk. In Bridlington (C9) the bells of the Priory Church were deliberately rung by the Church authorities to interrupt Wesley's sermon in the churchyard. Not to be deterred, he moved on to the market place of the old town and also preached at nearby Bridlington quay near the modern town centre. It is believed that Wesley once spent a night at Hunmanby Hall, near Filey, which later became a Methodist school for girls, now closed and re-developed as modern luxury apartments. Wesley once described the preaching house in Scarborough (C8) as 'the most elegant of any square room we have in England'. This Methodist chapel can be seen on Westborough, a few doors away from the birthplace of former Hollywood film actor Charles Laughton. Scarborough, a popular holiday resort, is dominated by its ruined Norman castle on a headland between two sweeping bays with splendid views along the rugged coastline as far as Flamborough Head to the south and Cloughton Wyke in a northerly direction.

Wesley also preached to fisher-folk at picturesque Robin Hood's Bay and Whitby (C7). Here, he addressed his flock on the steep hill with its famous 199 steps leading to the ruined Whitby Abbey (which later inspired Bram Stoker's vampire novel, *Dracula*), the green above St Mary's parish church, and also in the market place below, still full of maritime character with its ancient butter cross (a regular location in the Heartbeat television series). Moving inland to Guisborough, the story goes that John Wesley was provided with a table to stand on to preach in the market place. However, there was such a strong smell of fish that he almost suffocated.

While in North Yorkshire, though rather off the beaten track, the visitor should try and see the Methodist chapel in the hamlet of Osmotherley (C6) which nestles at the foot of the North York Moors and is the starting point for the 42-mile (68 km) Lyke Wake Walk long distance footpath to Ravenscar on the Yorkshire coast. The chapel dates from 1754. Wesley visited Osmotherley on 18 occasions, the first being at the invitation of a Roman

Catholic Franciscan friar. He sometimes stayed and preached at the Old Hall (now a Benedictine monastery, open daily) and also preached both in the parish church and outdoors from a stone table by the village cross. The lovely old market town of Richmond (c4) was another calling place and Wesley paid six visits. On at least one occasion he preached in the street named Newbiggin from the steps of an imposing town house, today called Christmas House, which stands opposite the Unicorn Hotel. The event is commemorated by a plaque. (This area has gained fame over recent years through the television series *All Creatures Great and Small* and films based on the novels of James Herriot.) Such North Yorkshire places were regular calling points for John Wesley on his way north to Newcastle-upon-Tyne to visit the many societies which had sprung up in the North-East of England.

# CHAPTER 11

# The North-East

RIDING NORTHWARDS, WESLEY used several routes during his years of itinerant preaching. In better weather he would have ventured into many of the northern dales but in spring or autumn was more likely to have chosen the flatter routes to the east or west of the Pennines. In Wesley's day the dales were remote places, difficult environments, a place where generations of hill farmers and lead miners had tried to make a living. Lead mining was instrumental in fashioning the character of the people involved in it. With a lack of pastoral oversight by Anglican Church authorities, these areas became a breeding ground for Nonconformism. Baptists, Quakers, Presbyterians and Congregationalists built their chapels around the Yorkshire dales and these older Dissenting traditions provided a sound basis for Methodism to thrive.

On reaching the River Tees, Wesley sometimes called to preach at an unusual Methodist chapel just off the high street in Yarm (C5), not far from Stockton-on-Tees. It was built in 1763 and is known to be the oldest octagonal chapel in the world still used by Methodists.

Crossing into County Durham, John Wesley occasionally took the road west through Teesdale to Alston, the highest market town in England and setting for the recent television serialisation of *Oliver Twist*. In May 1752, whilst preaching in Barnard Castle, a mob seized the local fire engine and sprayed water over Wesley's open-air congregation. Sometimes he rode on to Middleton-in-Teesdale and Newbiggin-in-Teesdale (B25) where there is a small Methodist chapel, built 1759 by lead miners and believed to be the oldest in the world to have remained in continuous use (a plaque was unveiled in 1996 acknowledging this). The village grew to prominence with the arrival of the London Lead Company in 1753. Amongst exhibits in the chapel are a display of Methodism and local history, including lead mining, and a former two-stage pulpit used by Wesley on several occasions. Of particular interest are the Bibles and Sunday School books of the London Lead Company, circuit plans and other memorabilia. Wesley's preachers first came to Teesdale in 1747 and the chapel was opened in 1760 to serve the first generation of Methodists. Most of Wesley's other congregations in Teesdale were composed of lead miners and, on one visit, he was taken to see the spectacular High Force waterfall, thought to be the highest in England, where the River Tees plunges seventy feet (21m) into a basin below. Indeed, some of the loveliest stretches of the Pennine Way pass nearby.

It is only a few miles from Newbiggin Chapel, which is open on Wednesday afternoons during summer months, to a similar building at Ireshopeburn (B24) in Weardale, the next northern dale. Wesley's first visit to Weardale was on 26 May 1752 where he preached near a thorn bush in Ireshopeburn. By the time of his second visit on 8 June 1761 the community had raised sufficient funding to erect a 'meeting house' for divine worship – High House Chapel – on land bought by John Emmerson of Hotts. Ten years later the chapel experienced a 'Revival of the Spirit' which greatly pleased Wesley who, in total, visited on 13 occasions, the last being in June 1790 when he was 86. 'This is country where the fires of Methodism took hold, fanned by absentee Anglicanism' he wrote. adjacent to the chapel is the splendid Weardale Museum which has a room dedicated to John Wesley with a fine collection of Methodist memorabilia and local history displays. An 1870 period Weardale cottage also forms part of the site which is open every afternoon during summer months except Monday and Tuesday and well worth a visit. Higher up the dale is the Killhope Lead Mining Centre, where visitors are taken back to the days of the once great lead mining industry.

Whilst travelling on horseback from one place to another, Wesley always made good use of his time by reading the scriptures, planning his next few sermons, sometimes in prayer or perhaps writing occasional notes. This would often be the case when travelling over many of the old drove roads and tracks across the barren northern terrain to reach his destination. His message was plain and clear for all to understand – 'Salvation for all through faith in God!'

The place to go to get a 'taste' of north-eastern culture is Beamish – the North of England Open Air Museum (B21). It is situated in 121 hectares of woodland and farmland, and illustrates the way of life in the area during the 19th and early 20th centuries. There are houses, shops, cottages and workshops along streets which have been created by the relocation of buildings from former sites and peopled by costumed characters and guides. There is both a steam railway and a tram track to connect with the various sites. Beamish has been used on a regular basis for filming television dramas set in the north-east, especially the adaptations of Catherine Cookson's novels. Of special interest is a Wesleyan Methodist chapel, dating from 1854, which once stood in the village of Pithill before being relocated to Beamish (a regular programme of singing by Methodist choirs takes place here during the summer). Close by are a coal mine, miners' cottages and a school.

Coal mining was very much a feature of the north-east and Wesley often preached to groups of miners and their families in pit villages such as Pelton, South Biddick and Chowden, now a suburb of Gateshead. To get there he would pass through the beautiful university city of Durham (B23) with its towering Norman cathedral, seat of the powerful Prince Bishops who ruled the area for centuries, standing sentinel over the meandering River Wear. The earliest inhabitants of the site were the monks of Lindisfarne who, from fear of Danish invaders, had moved the body of St Cuthbert (634-687) from its original tomb to a new resting place in the year AD 999. (The cathedral was the setting for scenes from the recent film Elizabeth). John Wesley often preached in the town and, in May 1780, visited Durham Castle, the residence of the bishop. He was more impressed with the view across the nearby cathedral and valley of the River Wear than the drab décor, furniture, other contents he found inside.

Charles Wesley was the original pioneer of Methodism in Sunderland (B22) after he rode over to preach from Newcastle on 16 June 1743. His congregation appeared reasonably attentive as the town already had a strong Nonconformist tradition which helped Methodism get established. (The town was both a port and industrial centre with visiting keel boats and sailing ships. Chapels had already been erected in the area by other Dissenting groups.) John visited two months after his brother on 11 July 1743 though he met with some hostility when preaching in the High Street. Matters improved and Wesley began to make an impression on the local population. However, he strongly disapproved of and preached against one of the local weaknesses – that of smuggling which had almost become a way of life in Sunderland and other coastal towns.

Newcastle-upon-Tyne (B20), the largest port in the north-east, became the main centre of Methodism in the region. Shipbuilding and coalmining were its main industries and John Wesley first entered the town with John Taylor, a servant of the Countess of Huntingdon, whom she had sent to act as a guide. They approached Newcastle from across the ancient medieval bridge over the River Tyne on 28 May 1742 and found the place full of drunkenness, cursing and swearing. Yet, determinedly, Wesley decided he would preach the following Sunday in Sandgate, one of the poorest and most thickly inhabited parts of the town. At frequent intervals narrow lanes called 'chares' led from the river, tightly lined with houses and lodgings. A crowd soon gathered and John promised to preach again later in the day just below Keelman's Hospital, later to become an early Methodist base, on a grassy bank known as 'Lousy Hill' because of the loafers lounging there. A Victorian obelisk, recently refurbished, was erected on the site at Sandgate near the old milk market on the modern Quayside immediately in front of the Newcastle Law Courts – the area has been renamed Wesley Square to commemorate Wesley's first preaching on Tyneside.

The society soon reached a strength of eight hundred and Wesley bought a piece of land on what is now Northumberland Street and built the Orphan House – his 'northern corner stone'. The foundation stone was laid on 20 December 1742 and a blue plaque marks the site on the fascia of Barratt's shoe shop in Northumberland Street. It was to become a base for John's future visits. The Orphan House served as a Sunday School, day school and lodging house for Methodist preachers and John had his study in the roof space. The building was demolished in 1856 and replaced by Wesleyan Schools. Several artefacts of Methodist history including a tea service and wall clock believed to have been used by Wesley at the Orphan House can be seen at nearby Brunswick Methodist Church in Brunswick Place. This church, which was built in 1820 and contains other Methodist memorabilia, is open to visitors on most days. Other places of Methodist interest in Newcastle are All Saints Church, to the east of the Tyne Bridge, built in 1796, where John and Charles often worshipped, and the Keelman's Hospital in whose square they regularly preached. In the churchyard of St Andrew's Church, Newgate Street, is the family tomb of William Smith, a preacher and founder trustee of the Orphan House. He was married to Jane Vazeille, who was one of John Wesley's two step-daughters.

## Grace Murray

It was in Newcastle where John Wesley experienced perhaps the greatest love of his life in the form of Grace Murray. She was married at only twenty to Alexander Murray and left a widow five years later. Earlier she had angered her husband by becoming a Methodist and female worker amongst the sick and poor of London, based at Wesley's Foundery Chapel. After her husband's death she returned to her mother's home in Newcastle and continued as a speaker and home visitor amongst women of the north-east. It was not long before she was appointed housekeeper at the Orphan House, where some of her duties were to take care of sick preachers, one of whom was John Bennet. The two started

*The Orphan House,*
*Newcastle-upon-Tyne*

to correspond with each other. When John Wesley fell ill while in the Newcastle area, he was also nursed by Grace. He soon began to feel that she was his ideal, became infatuated with her and, shortly afterwards, proposed marriage. Grace hesitated but asked if she could accompany him on his travels. On their journeys together they met up again in Chinley, Derbyshire, with John Bennet. For a short while Wesley left them together and Bennet started to woo Grace again and asked if there was anything between her and Wesley. 'No!' was her reply 'provided Mr. Wesley will give his consent, I will yield.' A letter was despatched to John Wesley immediately to which he only gave a mild response to the pair. But Grace did not really know her own mind.

In February 1749 Grace accompanied Wesley to Ireland for four months where she worked amongst women in smaller societies and visited the sick and dying. John Wesley's love for her was rekindled and in Dublin they were betrothed by a verbal contract, legally binding before the 1753 Marriage Act. When they returned to Bristol, Grace heard some untruths about a relationship John was supposed to have been having with a lady named Molly Francis. In a fit of jealousy she wrote to Bennet and asked him to meet her at Epworth on her journey north. Though still declaring she loved Wesley, she agreed to become Bennet's wife. Wesley returned to Newcastle and Grace then decided she wanted to marry him, not Bennet, immediately. Still he hesitated and wrote to his brother Charles Wesley for his permission. In turn, Charles rushed to Newcastle to raise his objection to the marriage. He met up with Grace and John Bennet and in less than a week they were married at St Andrew's Parish Church, Newcastle, in the presence of Charles along with George Whitefield. John Wesley had finally missed his opportunity though he did continue to work with Bennet as a preacher for a time. It led to a serious but temporary rift between the two Wesley brothers.

\* \* \*

In 1748 John Wesley made his first tour of the eastern and northern parts of Northumberland, now known again as Northumbria. It was his twelfth visit to the north-east. Prior to this he had concentrated his efforts on Newcastle and the Tyne and Wear areas. Northumberland Methodists had requested that he visit their societies and so John set out to meet some of these communities. He preached at the cross in Morpeth's market square (B19) then rode on to Widdrington, some nine miles north-east. He then went on to Alnmouth and to Alnwick (B18), one of the county's largest towns where he again preached at a market cross. The congregation was not very responsive. A chapel was built in 1786 with an adjoining manse and is still in use for worship. At that time Alnwick Castle was ruinous but soon to be rebuilt in its present form by the 1st Duke of Northumberland. From Alnwick, John rode up the Great North Road, preaching in the market place in Wooler, then on to Berwick-upon-Tweed (B17), a fortified town on the Scottish border.

On the coastal route he would have seen Bamburgh Castle in its precipitous setting on a rocky escarpment and then Holy Island, where St Aidan first brought Christianity to Northumbria in 635. On arrival in Berwick Wesley asked the commander of the garrison if he could use a piece of open ground to preach, and permission was granted. Afterwards, he turned south to return to Newcastle, on the way preaching at Tughall, Alnwick and Longhorsley. John Wesley made several other visits to Alnwick when travelling back from Scotland. Meanwhile, his ministry continued to flourish in England's most northerly county.

CHAPTER 12

# The West Country, Isle of Wight
# and Channel Islands

JOHN WESLEY WAS A regular visitor to the south-west of England and undoubtedly it was one of his favourite regions. Bristol was the base for his many journeys across the counties of Dorset, Wiltshire, Somerset, Devon and Cornwall and in the latter a particularly strong Methodist fraternity developed.

From Bristol, John often took the road to Taunton and stopped there on 22 occasions, the first being on 26 August 1743 when he preached in the open air at the market cross, now known as the Parade. At that time the place was filthy and overcrowded with a mixture of public houses and other buildings. By 1772 the place had been cleared and the market house built. (Taunton, nestling on the banks of the River Tone, is the county town of Somerset and dates back to Saxon times. It has had a turbulent past and featured in many a bloody uprising, the most famous being the Monmouth Rebellion of 1685 which ended in Judge Jeffreys' infamous Bloody Assize which was held in the great hall of the castle.) After four weeks John Wesley retraced his steps and stayed the night at the Three Cups Inn, now the County Hotel, in East Street which once boasted room for twenty carriages and stabling for one hundred horses.

The early Taunton Methodists met at the home of David Burford, whose house was licensed for preaching in July 1774. They used this building until the opening of their Octagon Chapel, just off Middle Street, two years later. It was opened by Wesley on 6 March 1776 when he was assisted by one of his Cornish preachers, John Murlin, who was later to be buried in the same vault as Wesley at the City Road Chapel, London. Over recent years the Octagon, no longer a chapel, has been expertly refurbished but is now surrounded by a private housing organisation and only visible in part through two openings. It is not open to the public.

A few months later, Wesley was back in Taunton when he travelled to nearby Kingston St Mary where he met Dr Thomas Coke, the Anglican curate from South Petherton in the rolling hills of Somerset, some twenty miles away. Wesley rode to spend the night with his friend the Rev James Brown at his parsonage on the hill beyond the churchyard. Between 1764-91, Brown was rector of St Peter's Church in Portishead near Bristol and was also one of the Countess of Huntingdon's chaplains. In addition, he held the living of Kingston St Mary. On arrival there, Wesley found Coke, a young Welsh clergyman, waiting to meet him. It was to prove a momentous occasion.

## Dr Thomas Coke

Thomas Coke was born in the little town of Brecon in South Wales in 1747 where he attended schools before going on to Jesus College, Oxford. He graduated in 1768 and was awarded a doctorate of Law in 1775. Like the Wesley brothers he was ordained Deacon in Christ Church Cathedral and went on to be ordained priest at Abergwili near Carmarthen in 1772. There is a memorial tablet to Dr Coke in Brecon Cathedral. By the time he met Wesley he was almost 29 and the old gentleman of 73 advised him to continue in the same path as a curate. Despite this, he began to preach and practice a Christianity which cared for the underprivileged and ignored the aristocracy. Soon, villagers and ruffians hounded Coke out of Church and village. They even threw stones at him and the church bells in South Petherton (E9) were rung in celebration of his departure. As a result, Coke was dismissed from his living at South Petherton and joined up with the Methodists. Soon his powers of leadership and organisation became obvious and John Wesley started to depend on him in many areas. He began to see Coke as his own possible successor to the leading position in establishing the Methodist Church.

On 2 September 1784 at No. 6 Dighton Street in Bristol, Wesley ordained Thomas Coke as the Superintendent of the rapidly growing work of Methodism in America. Dr Coke was, in turn, to lay his own hands on Francis Asbury at the Christmas Conference in 1784 held in Baltimore to ordain him as first bishop of the American Methodist Church. Dr Thomas Coke is also the man to whom the setting-up of the Methodist Missionary Society can be attributed. He died at sea on 2 May 1814 and his body was committed to the Indian Ocean.

\* \* \*

South Petherton was once of great strategic importance on the Fosse Way. This compact little hamstone town has many small shops and a quiet unhurried charm about it. The fine parish church of St Peter and St Paul where Coke was once curate has an octagonal central tower and is well worth a visit. Its origins were Early English but most of the church was rebuilt in the Perpendicular style in the 15th century. The crossing between the nave and chancel contains some fine vaulting with corbels of the four descending groins bearing symbols of the four Evangelists. The area has been filled with choir stalls in beautiful English woodcarving. They were given in 1935 by Methodist laymen in memory of Dr Thomas Coke, curate of the parish from 1771-77 and the house where he lived in nearby St James Street is marked by a plaque. It was in North Street that the first Methodist chapel opened in 1808 but the present building was built in 1882 at the end of St James's Street as a centenary memorial to Dr Coke. John Wesley preached in South Petherton on 3 September 1778.

Five days later John preached in the market place at Frome, Somerset, where he found his congregation 'very gentlemanly'. Frome market place is little-changed today from the 18th century and it retains a number of original buildings. The first Methodist chapel was opened on the present site in 1779 and replaced in 1812 during the course of a great Revival. John called to see his mother, Susanna, in both March and June 1738, after she had taken up residence for a short time in Salisbury, Wiltshire (E11). It was also Francis Asbury's final circuit before he set sail for America in September 1771. Wesley preached in Salisbury at a shop in Greencroft Street, at nearby Harnham Hill, and also other local sites and surrounding towns such as Devizes, Melksham and Trowbridge to name but a few. He took the opportunity to visit and admire the wonderful Cathedral in Salisbury, completed in the 13th century by Bishop Richard Poore. The tower and spire, a combined height of 404 ft (123 m), the tallest in England, were added in 1334. The visitor to Salisbury should also take a look at the nearby Cathedral Close, the largest and finest in Britain. It is entered through medieval gateways, and many of the buildings inside, such as the Bishop's Palace and the Deanery, are also medieval. Some private residences in the close date from later periods including the fine 18th century Mompesson House.

\* \* \*

Poole, on the south coast of England, was then the largest town in Dorset. It had strong family links with John Wesley, his grandfather, John, being the town's first Independent minister after losing his living at Winterbourne Whitechurch in 1662. Wesley also took in the dramatic ruins of Corfe Castle en route to Swanage and, in the small village of Corfe, preached at a place known as Well Court, a courtyard of stone houses at 18-22 West Street, opposite the post office. He also preached in a nearby field. Few castles in England can rival the setting of Corfe Castle as it towers above the village from its hilltop site. It seems to guard a natural passageway in a ridge of the Purbeck Hills, and was built by William the Conqueror. During the Civil Wars it became the last Royalist stronghold between London and Devon and was eventually bombarded by Cromwell.

John visited nearby Swanage (E12) in October 1774, preached in a field, and stayed the night at Burts' cottage which once stood next to the Town Hall. On one occasion in 1787, Wesley and Thomas Coke were travelling by boat to the Channel Islands from Southampton when a storm caused them to take shelter at Yarmouth on the Isle of Wight where Wesley preached twice in the market place. (Both John and Charles were on the island in 1735. They arrived at St Helen's harbour and the following day went on to Cowes. By 1753 a Methodist society had been formed in Newport (E14), the chief town, where John preached in the market place. Later, on 10 October 1781, he opened the newly-completed chapel there.) A favourable wind which enabled them to restart developed into a storm which drove them into Swanage Bay. They were given shelter in the town of Swanage by the Presbyterian minister who allowed John to preach in his chapel. The hall, built in 1705, adjacent to the present United Reformed Church, is the building in which Wesley preached in this charming resort on the spectacular Dorset coast.

\* \* \*

Eventually, they were able to continue their journey and landed at Alderney in the Channel Islands on 14 August 1787. They stayed one night in the Divers' Inn, which was wrecked during German raids in the Second World War but rebuilt in the 1950s. John also preached in Alderney on Braye Sands to a large gathering who sang hymns. (A tablet in the foyer of Alderney Methodist Church commemorates Wesley's visit to the island.)

Next day they arrived in Guernsey where John preached at St Peter Port in a large room of Mr Henri de Jersey's house, Mont Plaisir les Terres, situated on the edge of the town at St Jacques. John later addressed a large congregation in a Methodist chapel at the opposite end of the town. On the following day he had a conversation with the island's Governor and, later, he and Coke dined with him.

Their next port of call was Jersey. They landed at St Helier and went straight to see John's old friend and fellow preacher from Lincolnshire, Robert Brackenbury, who lived at No. 15 Old Street. Wesley had sent Brackenbury to do his work in the Channel Islands and John stayed with him whilst he preached in the town. He also attended a service at the local parish church. Two days later they travelled to St Mary's on the northern side of the same island where John preached in a house called Le Marais on the text 'By grace are ye saved, through faith'. He returned to Guernsey where he was offered the use of the Assembly Room (the present Guille-Allès Library), a spacious building in the market place. In total Wesley stayed three weeks in the Channel Islands and his visit revitalised the various congregations. Yet opposition to his methods and teachings began to take root amongst the local parishes.

## Samuel Wesley Junior

Tiverton (E8) in Devon was a regular calling place for John Wesley, not only for preaching but for visiting his elder brother, Samuel, who was headmaster of Old Blundell's School until 1739. The School was built by wealthy wool merchant Peter Blundell in 1604 as a gift to the people of Tiverton. Its former pupils include the much-loved Archbishop Frederick Temple and RD Blackmore, author of the novel *Lorna Doone*. The sandstone slate-roofed school is described in the book which opens in the forecourt of Old Blundell's. In 1882 the building was converted into houses but is now in the hands of the National Trust. However, the public are only allowed access to the forecourt.

Samuel Wesley Jnr died on 5 November 1739 and is buried in the churchyard of St George's Church, Tiverton, one of the finest Georgian churches in Devon, situated at the junction of St Andrew's and St Peter's Streets, opposite the Town Hall. The church was erected between 1714-30, largely by voluntary subscriptions, and is a plain building of Purbeck stone. Unfortunately, it is not possible to locate Samuel's exact burial place but the gravestone has since been set into the outside rear wall of St George's. An alleyway passes the memorial and leads to the excellent Tiverton Museum which can assist visitors with more specific details.

\* \* \*

It was around the time of brother Samuel's funeral that John Wesley preached his first morning sermon in Exeter (E6), probably at St Mary Major's Church. He was not allowed to preach in the afternoon. On a later occasion, on 18 August 1782 John attended worship in Exeter Cathedral and was invited by the Bishop to have dinner in the adjacent Palace. Wesley described the meal as 'sufficient but not redundant; plain and good, but not delicate'. Other places at which John sometimes called included Cullompton, Crediton and Tavistock, occasionally taking the packhorse routes across Dartmoor. Plymouth (E5) had long been a seat of Nonconformity (the town had earlier rallied to help the Pilgrim Fathers in September 1620 when they put in to Sutton Pool Harbour for repairs to one of their ships, the *Speedwell*, which should have accompanied the *Mayflower* to America). Wesley preached in the square by the harbourside, near to the Pilgrims' departure point, on 18 August 1782, and paid several other visits to the town.

* * *

Cornwall's landscape is scarred with the traces of both ancient and modern mineral extraction. Noticeable today are the remains of mine engine-houses which are dotted around the Cornish landscape. These relics are of an industry which in the late 18th century made the county one of the foremost tin and copper producers in the world. Many small mining villages developed on former moorland or heath and ports often became important industrial centres in their own right. As in other parts of the country, there was a movement of population from rural areas to the new industrial centres. This was the scenario when Wesley first arrived in Cornwall. He came to minister to these growing neighbourhoods, mainly populated by tin and copper miners and their families. Nonconformism had already started to take root in the area but it was Wesley and his preachers who made the greatest impact upon its residents.

There was something magnetic which drew Wesley to Cornwall – the 'end of England' and on more than one occasion he scrambled down the rocks at Land's End. In 1743 he sailed in a fishing boat to the Isles of Scilly, accompanied by John Nelson, and landed at St Mary's where they presented the Governor with a copy of the *Sherborne Mercury*, the only newspaper circulating in Cornwall at the time. The local vicar would not allow John to use his church so he preached in the street. Many local people and military men attended.

John was also a frequent visitor to St Just, where he preached by the church gate and on the Plen-an-Gwary nearby – where medieval plays were once acted. Wesley's host in St Just was the innkeeper William Chenhalls, whose house still stands opposite the parish church gate. Leaving by the road to St Ives, one passes a small hamlet called Rosemergy where two more of Wesley's hosts, John and Alice Daniel, once lived. It is mentioned four times in Wesley's Journal. Beyond is the small village of Zennor where John preached 'under the churchyard wall' but it was John Nelson, the Yorkshire preacher, his companion in 1743, who preached from a prominent granite outcrop called Trewey Rock on the right of the lane leading to Zennor Church – not John Wesley as many believed. Wesley's host in Zennor was Matthew Thomas whose tombstone can be seen at the church.

Arriving in the popular holiday town of St Ives (E1) with its glorious bays, sandy beaches, quaint cottages, alleyways and a multitude of steps which snake up and down the hillside, one can be forgiven for thinking we are not in the 21st century. The visitor is brought swiftly back to reality when we see the modern Tate St Ives and Barbara Hepworth Museum with contemporary works of art and abstract paintings. For years St Ives has housed a colony of artists, painters and sculptors. The sculptress, Barbara Hepworth, lived there along with other well-known Bohemian and artistic characters who together created an outpost for the abstract avant-garde.

St Ives was a mining centre in the 18th century and both Wesleys faced opposition in the town during the early years. In

1744 a number of attacks were made on Methodist meetings in Cornwall by local mobs. St Ives was no exception. A tablet on the outside wall of Wesley's Chapel in the town records that the house of John Nance, Wesley's host, once stood across the lane. The doorway by this tablet and the walling around, are parts of the chapel, rebuilt in 1785, in which John preached. According to tradition, there was an occasion when, anxious to get to his destination, Wesley ordered his carriage to be driven through the sea. At the time the sands between Hayle and St Ives were being encroached upon by the rising tide, and the horses had to swim.

On the south Cornish coast, Wesley preached on the Western Green at Penzance in 1747 and had to be rescued from an unruly mob which had gathered. The green was an open space running alongside the coastline between Penzance and Newlyn. One mile away in Heamoor is Wesley Rock Chapel which possesses a pulpit that stands on top of a block of granite from which Wesley preached when it stood in a nearby field. At Gulval, also near Penzance, is a memorial in the chancel of the parish church commemorating Philothea Briggs, one of Wesley's lady correspondents, the 'Dear Philly' of his letters. Whilst in the area in 1745 John paid a visit to the romantic but remote St Michael's Mount in lovely Mount's Bay while waiting to attend a magistrate's court at Marazion. Following his encounter with an unruly crowd at Falmouth in 1745, Wesley's friends, fearing further trouble, arranged for his horse to go on to Penrhyn while he himself was smuggled through a house which backed on to the waterfront and then went on to Penrhyn by boat to be re-united with his mount. It was a lucky escape.

Just a few miles up the west Cornish coast from St Ives, near to Hayle, is the small hamlet of Gwithian (E1) which boasts the only remaining thatched chapel still in existence in Cornwall. The chapel was built in 1810. An old agreement states 'that visiting preachers still have the right to stable their horses in the yard of the Pendarves Arms Hotel'. Wesley rode through Gwithian in 1757 with Thomas Harris of Rosewarne who pointed out where his ancestors had once lived prior to their homes being engulfed by encroaching sands. Nearby, the Atlantic rollers pound their way over the precipitous rocks of Hell's Mouth.

John regularly preached at the entrance to the market house in Fore Street in the nearby town of Redruth as well as from the balcony at Bank House, West End. He also worshipped at St Euny's Church both before and after its rebuilding in 1756. Well worth a visit is Carharrack Methodist Church, approximately four miles from Redruth, which houses the Museum of Cornish Methodism (E2). The church itself dates from 1815 with an impressive interior and ornate pulpit. There are many artefacts relating to the life of John Wesley up to his arrival in Cornwall in 1743 and other Methodist preachers. There is also information about other local leaders and the various denominations which now make up the Methodist Church. Plans are in hand for the exhibits to be moved to a purpose-built museum at Gwennap Pit.

Gwennap Pit (E2) is less than a mile from Carharrack and one of Methodism's most unusual sites. The Pit originated from the collapse of old tin mine workings which created a large green hollow. It was first discovered by Wesley in 1762 and soon became his favourite open air preaching place in Cornwall. A grassy open air amphitheatre with excellent accoustic properties, it was ideal for preaching and John went to the Pit on eighteen

*Gwennap Pit*

occasions between 1762-89, always on a Sunday afternoon. In 1806 work commenced on remodeling the Pit into its present form as a memorial to John Wesley. It has an upturned conical appearance in steps leading down to a central pivot. As a further memorial to John, a set of artistically designed concrete and mosaic panels by Guy Sanders were erected some years ago. These relate Wesley's message and tell the story of Gwennap Pit, together with the small visitor centre nearby. The Pit, one of the most photographed sites in Methodism, is open daily and, following the Spring Bank Holiday service, afternoon meetings are held each Sunday during July and August. It is quite a moving experience to attend.

## The Bible Christians – William O'Bryan and Billy Bray

It was in this area of Cornwall where the founder of another breakaway group of Methodists grew up. This group, known as the Bible Christians, was founded by William O'Bryan (1778-1868) whose first society class was held at Shebbear (E7) near Beaworthy in North Devon. He was born in the parish of Luxulyan, Cornwall, where he grew up at Gunwen and served as Churchwarden. He later built a chapel on land he had purchased in 1820 at Innis near Lanivet in the Bodmin area of Cornwall. Artefacts relating to O'Bryan's life and other Bible Christian memorabilia can be seen in the chapel. The heartland of this group was centred on north-east Cornwall and north-west Devon. Rather like the Primitive Methodists – another breakaway group – they had many women itinerant preachers during their early days.

One of the most famous Bible Christians was Billy Bray (1794-1868) who was an original preacher and wit. He was a tin miner, a well-known evangelist, and a builder of chapels – the best known being Billy Bray's Chapel at Kerley Downs, Chacewater. The chapel and obelisk in Baldhu Churchyard are his memorials. This chapel was once known as Three Eyes because it originally had three windows. Above the pulpit is a print of a painting of

Billy Bray. (Other artefacts relating to the Bible Christians are on display in the Cornish Museum of Methodism at Carharrack.) Kerley Downs Chapel is open daily from June to September.

In 1841 Billy Bray was one of the preachers at the opening of a much enlarged chapel for the Bible Christians at Shebbear – where the first Bible Christian society had begun. It was known as Lake Chapel and could accommodate two hundred people and provide the sect with a place to hold their own annual conference. The site also included a proprietary school – later called Shebbear College – and a farm. In 26 years the Bible Christians built over three hundred chapels and recruited almost 12,000 members. It was not however until 1907 that they became part of the new United Methodist Church and, by that time, they had spread to other parts of England with a total membership of 100,000. Shebbear College is now a Methodist independent school and open during term time with viewing by arrangement.

\* \* \*

Truro (E3) is a cathedral city and the cultural, commercial and administrative centre of Cornwall with a history going back a thousand years. It was heavily involved in the Civil War, being strongly Royalist, and in 1642 the town raised a large army to fight for Charles I. However, four years later it fell to the Roundhead Fairfax and the King had to make a quick escape via Falmouth. Because of its strategic position close to the Truro and Fal rivers, the town became an important port and tin mining centre. The cathedral itself, the building of which began in 1880 and took thirty years, dominates the town with three fine towers and spires which soar grandly to the sky with gabled dormers and pinnacles like traceried spirelets. The central steeple, climbing 250 ft (76 m) – a foot for every mile the city is from London – is Cornwall's memorial to Queen Victoria. It was, in fact, the first cathedral to be built in England since St Paul's in London. The lofty West Front faces a small square and in the cathedral are a number of Methodist associations. Perhaps the most obvious is the Wesley Window, a lancet window in the south aisle of the nave showing Wesley preaching at Gwennap Pit. He is also depicted in a group with his brother Charles and Samuel Walker, the evangelical and Calvinistic curate of Truro, seated at his feet. John did not form the society in the town until Walker left the parish. He preached in Boscawen Street close to the present war memorial and also by West Bridge, now Victoria Square. The most commanding Methodist Church in the city today is St Mary Clement, built 1830, which has an imposing Grecian style frontage.

Wesley travelled the length and breadth of Cornwall many times, preaching at numerous wayside places. A favourite stopping place was Trewint (E4) at what is today known as Wesley's Cottage (signposted off theA30 at Five Lanes). In the early 18th century it was the home of stonemason Digory Isbell and his wife Elizabeth. They welcomed Wesley's preachers, John Nelson and John Downes, a Northumbrian, in 1743 and on later occasions John himself was their guest. Digory added a wing to his cottage containing an upper and lower room which Wesley and his preachers could use at any time. John often preached from the stone porch as indeed preachers still do at annual Wesley Day services on 24 May. A small society was formed in this area of Cornwall which met regularly at the cottage. Today the 18th century building, refurbished in contemporary style, offers a warm welcome to visitors and houses a small display of Methodist memorabilia in the 'upper' room. It is open daily and has a wonderful atmosphere of solitude - especially in the room where Wesley and his preachers prayed so long ago. The graves of Digory and Elizabeth Isbell can be seen in the churchyard of the nearby pretty village of Altarnun, set in a hollow on the edge of Bodmin Moor. Over the doorway of the old chapel is a half-relief head of Wesley carved by sculptor Nevil Northy Burnard. Other regular stopping points for John Wesley in Cornwall included Camelford, Port Isaac, Goldsithney, St Austell, Bodmin, Launceston, Liskeard and Polperro. In total, he made 32 visits to the county between 1743 and 1789.

The area undoubtedly provided spiritual refreshment for Wesley and his preachers as they journeyed around England to spread the Gospel of Jesus Christ.

# CHAPTER 13

# Matrimonial Instability

THE JOURNALS AND LETTERS of John Wesley prove that women as well as men were drawn to the great preacher. His prime attraction was as a leader and man of God but one should not underestimate the extent to which women were attracted by his manly principles. Wesley was also a great letter writer and the author of many tracts, books and publications and, through his brilliant organisation, these were sold or distributed through his national network of preachers and other lay workers. He wrote on a variety of subjects, usually with a Biblical theme. Sometimes he would write on other issues, as in *A Thought Upon Marriage* which he published in 1785. It could almost have been a post mortem on his own unsuccessful attempts at nuptial happiness.

From his early dalliance with Sophy Hopkey in Georgia, John Wesley had been unsuccessful in finding a partner to share his life. He was not without lady friends in various parts of the country with whom he conversed on a variety of religious and other subjects. He was welcomed into many close family circles or spiritual gatherings where he would undoubtedly have had ample opportunity to meet members of the opposite sex. Had he been more positive over his decision to wed Grace Murray and acted more decisively upon it, John might have made a successful marriage. However, his itinerant lifestyle would be a daunting prospect for any potential bride.

There is no doubt that John must have been envious of his brother Charles, and the happy marriage and family life he had created for himself. It was a happiness John also hoped to achieve. Within a week of Charles' marriage to Sarah Gwynne, John invited Grace Murray to accompany him to Ireland to share in his work. She accepted. The outcome of the relationship was, of course, that she eventually married John Bennet after intervention from Charles Wesley. John resolved that his brother would never again interfere in any of his matrimonial aspirations.

Shortly afterwards John had an accident on London Bridge when he slipped on the ice and badly sprained his ankle. He was due to leave shortly afterwards on a tour of the North but this had to be delayed. He took up quarters at the house in Threadneedle Street (A2) of Mrs Mary (Molly) Vazeille, a widow of Huguenot descent, who nursed him through his incapacity. Her late husband, a London merchant, had left her a wealthy woman. Whether or not he was on the rebound from the Grace Murray relationship, John, then aged 48, married Mrs Vazeille, aged 41, on 18 February 1751. In so doing he had to resign his Fellowship and income from Lincoln College. In order not be considered a fortune hunter, John settled ten thousand pounds worth of property on his wife and the children from her former marriage. The wedding seems to have been a very quiet affair.

The marriage took place largely through the encouragement of his brother Charles and friend Vincent Perronet, who both spoke well of Molly. Whereas over the Grace Murray episode John had been slow, on this occasion he moved much faster. John proposed, was accepted, and the couple were married within a week. There was perhaps no better proof of the saying – 'Marry in haste – repent at leisure'.

In the early months of marriage she travelled with John but soon found the mode of living rather wearying and uncomfortable due to the many journeys they had to make. This lifestyle involved travelling through all weathers, often at unsociable hours, to reach the various destinations where John was due to preach or attend meetings. It did not augur well for a successful marriage. Cracks soon began to appear in the relationship and rows started to take place between the couple. However, John Wesley's foremost priority was continuing with the Lord's work and this took absolute precedence over all other matters – especially those of a matrimonial nature. He would not compromise in his duty to his Christian calling and Molly, his wife, refused to accept this, often with uncontrolled rage and insults, both verbally and in the letters which passed between them. It was a downward spiral.

There are always two sides to any story and one cannot but have some sympathy for Molly Wesley. The long absences of John on his travels, the lack of any joint social life or constant mutual affection would all have taken their toll. These, coupled with the only prospect of being his constant travelling companion, would have weighed heavily against the marriage becoming a success. During the early days of marriage John wrote to his wife praising her for the work she was doing among the Methodist societies and of his concern for her spiritual welfare. addressing her as 'my dear love' he also wrote of the happiness he felt from 'his dearest earthly friend'. However, within three months of marriage, Molly first intimated in a letter to one of Wesley's friends that she had 'many trials'. By the end of the year she started to show signs of jealousy and was convinced that John no longer loved her. Her anger began to show in public and criticism of Wesley almost bordered on slander. Her true colours started to appear as her suspicious nature and possessiveness began to spill over into mental instability.

After nearly five years they decided to go their separate ways but to still keep in contact. John still hoped for a reconciliation even as late as 1777 after his wife had deserted him for Newcastle a few years earlier. It was not to be. Mrs Wesley continued to damage her husband's reputation by showing some of his private letters to others and accusing him of adultery with certain of his female correspondents. This of course was quite untrue, but for over twenty years she plagued him with her accusations, suspicions and untruths.

One of John's problems was the fact that his ties with his own mother, Susanna, had been extremely close. He was like her in temperament, had a logical approach, and possessed a penetrating mind. His mother had become his role model and he measured all women against the very high principles which Susanna had set for her children. Whoever he married would have found it difficult to achieve such exacting standards. There were also the heavy demands made by his calling to travel, to organise the various Methodist societies, and to preach the Gospel. These pressures would each have contributed to the break-up of the marriage. John must therefore have accepted some of the blame for the breakdown.

John Wesley wrote to his wife in October 1778 accusing her of slandering him and stating that, from his own point of view, the marriage was over. She died three years later on 8 October 1781 and was buried in the churchyard of St Giles in Camberwell, South London. The tombstone disappeared when a roadway was widened. The children of her married daughter are mentioned in John Wesley's will as 'my dear grand-daughters'.

# CHAPTER 14

# Wesley's Chapel, London

WHEN SUSANNA WESLEY first came to live at the Foundery in London in 1740, she discovered the building was in a somewhat dilapidated condition. However, she soon settled in and had the companionship of John between his journeys, Charles, who lived nearby, and some of her married daughters who had also gravitated towards the metropolis. She was able to discuss in some detail the religious experiences of her two sons and the work to which they had been called. It was not long before Susanna was also assisting with the work at the Foundery and she started to teach classes of women. John relied more and more on his mother to 'keep her eye' on matters during his regular absences.

As time went by Susanna became increasingly frail and was confined to bed. The end came on 23 July 1742 when she was 73 years of age. Apart from Charles who had left London on important business, all her children were present at her deathbed. Susanna Wesley was interred at the nearby Nonconformist burial ground of Bunhill Fields (A9). Under the Act of Uniformity of 1662 no Dissenters were allowed to be buried in any consecrated Anglican ground nor within the City of London. Bunhill Fields then stood just outside the old City boundary. Susanna's grave is of white marble stone and is visible some distance to the left of the central path. The burial ground also contains the graves of other Nonconformists such as Daniel Defoe, Isaac Watts, William Blake and John Bunyan. It is an oasis of serenity, yet only a stone throw from the bustle of London traffic on City Road.

The Foundery was John Wesley's London base for over thirty years from when it opened in December 1739. As well as a public place of worship he established other social facilities at the premises including a free school, for sixty students with two teachers, and a free medical clinic and dispensary, complete with an apothecary and surgeon. Two years later he rented an adjacent house as a refuge for widows and children. The first Methodist Conference was held at the Foundery by the Wesleys, four other clergymen and four lay preachers between 25-30 June 1744. By this institution Wesley was able to consolidate his movement and it provided a safety valve for differences of opinion. He undoubtedly retained a tight grip on the movement by fostering this annual practice. It was a means by which those in the Methodist church could keep in touch with each other and maintain a continuing evangelical witness. In British Methodism the Annual Conference has ultimate oversight over Districts and circuits and includes equal numbers of lay and ministerial representatives. It has overall control on matters of doctrine and policy.

A year earlier Wesley had opened two further churches in London. The first was at No. 26 West Street, off the Charing Cross Road, in a former French Protestant church, built circa 1700 (there is a commemorative plaque). The building was rented by the Wesleys and it became the headquarters of Methodist work in the West End of London until 1798. This former chapel stands next to the Ambassadors Theatre but is now under commercial usage. The second church opened in 1743 was at Snow's Field in Bermondsey, but has now disappeared. During the early years in London the Foundery buildings served John well but both time and the elements began to take their toll and much repair work became necessary. In any case the lease on the building was running out and local plans were in hand for residential development in the Moorfields area. Both John and Charles Wesley and other preachers delivered the Word of God in the open air around the Finsbury Square (A8) area of Moorfields. A new and larger place of worship was most desirable for the Methodists.

Across the lane from Bunhill Fields (which later became City Road) was a large piece of waste ground which had been reclaimed from former swamp land. In 1777 John Wesley rented an acre (0.4 hectares) of this land as the site for a new chapel to be built. On 21 April, in the presence of a large crowd, he laid the foundation stone of the new building. After eighteen months, on 1 November 1778, sufficient progress had been made on the chapel to allow public worship for the former congregation of the Foundery. Wesley preached both in the morning and afternoon and recorded in his Journal 'It is perfectly neat, but not fine; and contains far more people than the Foundery'. The front portico was added a few years later in 1815. (In all of Wesley's chapels the men sat apart from the women. Congregations were noted for their 'swift singing' without organ accompaniment'.)

Money had to be raised to finance the building of the Chapel and Wesley frequently asked for contributions from his various congregations during his preaching tours. King George III presented masts of warships from the docks at nearby Deptford. These were used to support the gallery and were covered in plaster and painted to give the impression of Carrara marble. They were kept for a century but then removed to the vestibule.

Originally the stairs to the gallery were inside the Chapel and there was no organ, the singing being led by a precentor. A certain number of the pews could be rented out to help defray expenses. Apart from the stained glass windows and many memorials, the Chapel is little changed from Wesley's day. A fire broke out in 1879 and destroyed most of the Adam-style ceiling which was reputed to be the widest unsupported ceiling in England when it was first built. Careful work was carried out to restore original features and the Chapel was re-opened for worship by the Methodist Conference of 1880. Eleven years later in 1891, the centenary of John Wesley's death, funding was raised to complete the renovation work. The foundations were set in concrete and the present oak pews were installed.

As one enters the forecourt of Wesley's Chapel (A10) from City Road through ornate wrought iron gates, one is confronted by a fine bronze statue of John Wesley clasping the Bible in one hand with the other raised in benediction. On the plinth is a quotation

*Wesley's Chapel, London*

which reads The World Is My Parish. The statue by Adams-Acton was erected in 1891.

On entering the vestibule, one sees some of the preserved wooden man o' war masts, presented by George III, which once supported the balcony. We then get our first glimpse of the interior of the main body of the Chapel. In the centre of the sanctuary is a fine mahogany pulpit, once a three-decker. The three-sided communion rail around the altar was presented to Wesley's Chapel by Sir Dennis and Baroness Margaret Thatcher, Britain's first woman Prime Minister, who were married in the building and also had their twins, Carol and Mark, baptized there. The original communion area was behind the pulpit, a tradition which has survived in Wesley's Chapel despite changes introduced by the Oxford Movement. There are numerous memorials around the walls and in the apse are those to John and Charles Wesley, John Fletcher, Dr Thomas Coke and two leading preachers, Joseph Benson and Adam Clarke. Stained glass windows include one dedicated to Bishop Francis Asbury, founding father of the American Methodist Church, and the font once belonged to John Fletcher's church at Madeley in

Shropshire. It contains a carving made from the pavement of the house in Antigua where the first Methodist class meeting in the West Indies was held.

To the right of the main chapel is a smaller one which has been re-named the Foundery Chapel to commemorate the original meeting place of the London Methodists, and is used for prayer and small services. It contains some old forms from the Foundery and also, in a recess, houses Charles Wesley's chamber organ on which members of his family played music to the many visitors they received at their home in nearby Marylebone High Street.

The Museum of Methodism (A10) occupies the crypt or basement area of Wesley's Chapel and covers the many facets of the Methodist Church, its history, and its growth both in Britain and on a worldwide basis. The Museum also contains items of personal effects which belonged to John Wesley and other early Methodist preachers.

Over the years Wesley's Chapel has often been called The Cathedral of World Methodism as it is in this building that many notable Methodist preachers, laymen, scholars and statesmen are recorded and honoured. In 1978, Her Majesty Queen Elizabeth II attended the re-opening of the Chapel after restoration. It is well known that many Methodist groups are renowned for their enthusiastic manner in the singing of hymns. On leaving the building Her Majesty was heard to comment 'I feel the Methodists really enjoy their singing!' 'They sing with such gusto' would probably have been a more apt description!

Adjacent to and part of Wesley's Chapel is the Leysian Centre which caters for social outreach. In addition, the splendid Museum of Methodism was opened in 1984. It traces the origins of 18th century Methodism and tells the ongoing story of its spread around the world, its work and achievements. It also houses special exhibitions which relate to Methodist, political or social themes. In particular is an excellent collection of Wesleyana pottery which includes busts of Wesley, jugs, plates, medallions and loving cups. Over the years, such items have been coveted by eager collectors and can command high prices.

To the right of the Chapel forecourt is Wesley's House (A10) on City Road, designed by George Dance to John Wesley's specifications and built by Samuel Tooth. John spent the first night in his new residence on 8 October 1779. It has a blue plaque fitted to the front of the building and he lived there during the last eleven years of his life. It is a rare example of a middle class 18th century London town house which has survived destruction or redevelopment, and was dedicated as a museum in 1898. The actual areas of the building occupied by John Wesley were the three first-floor rooms. The remaining floors were used by preachers of the London Methodist circuit. Today, the house is kept as it might have been in Wesley's day and includes many effects and items of Wesleyan memorabilia.

John Wesley died in his bedroom and this leads into a small room at the back of the house which is kept as a quiet room for prayer as this was where John started his day and retired to in order to study the Bible or be 'at peace with his Maker'. The room has sometimes been called the Power house of Methodism. The Queen Anne walnut table, study candlestick and chair all belonged to him. The room at the front of the house was Wesley's study and contains his library of books. An unusual exhibit is an electrical machine which he used at the Foundery for experiments in shock therapy for a variety of ailments. On the wall is a famous portrait of Wesley in later life, painted by Robert Hunter in 1765. Other effects, such as Wesley's preaching gown, tricorn hat, cravat, shoes and buckles, are displayed in the basement area of the house.

John Wesley's tomb is in the churchyard at the rear of the Chapel, now sadly overshadowed by a modern office development.

# CHAPTER 15

# Scotland

JOHN WESLEY FIRST ventured into Scotland in 1751 on the first of 22 visits spanning 39 years. He crossed the border at Berwick and rode northwards at the invitation of Captain Gallatin who was officer in charge of troops at Musselburgh (B15). Six years earlier Bonnie Prince Charlie had won a decisive victory over Hanoverian forces at nearby Prestonpans and Wesley saw the battle site as he passed by. However, the Jacobite cause was finally lost at the battle of Culloden which took place on 16 April 1746. The 'Young Pretender' – Bonnie Prince Charlie – had managed to escape to France and disillusionment. By the time of Wesley's first visit north of the border both Scotland and England were beginning to pick up the pieces after the Jacobite defeat. Amongst ordinary soldiers of government troops were some Methodists who were instrumental in starting societies in the places where they were stationed. One such group who had served in Flanders with the Dragoon Guards had already been established at Dunbar. They, like the Wesleys, had been influenced by the Moravians. A similar band of Methodist soldiers in Aberdeen drew attention to themselves by singing some of Charles Wesley's hymns.

Some of Wesley's itinerant preachers in northern England, notably Christopher Hopper, had already travelled into various parts of Scotland, especially to the more populated towns and cities of the Lowlands. It was therefore in Wesley's interest that he was seen to be supporting the work already begun in Scotland by his followers.

He arrived at Musselburgh, then a small burgh and port of the south bank of the River Forth, on 24 April. The following day he paid his first visit to Edinburgh (B14) which he describes in his

Journal for 11 May 1761 – 'the situation of the city, on a hill shelving down on both sides, as well as to the east, with the stately castle upon a craggy rock on the west, is inexpressibly fine. And the main street, so broad and finely paved, with the lofty houses on either hand (many of them seven or eight storeys high) is far beyond any in Great Britain. Holyroodhouse, the ancient palace of Scottish kings at the entrance of Edinburgh, is a noble structure. It was rebuilt by Charles II. One side of it is a picture gallery, housing paintings of all the Scottish Kings and an original one of the celebrated Queen Mary. It is hardly possible to look at this and believe her such a monster as some have painted her – especially for anyone who considers the circumstances of her death equal to those of an ancient martyr.

On other visits to Edinburgh John Wesley preached on the Castle Esplanade, in the High School Yards and on Calton Hill 'where the wind blew away a few delicate folk'. He also attended Holy Communion in the West Kirk now known as St Cuthbert's. Nicholson Square Methodist Church in Edinburgh is a classical church by Thomas Brown built in 1815-16, the successor of an earlier octagonal chapel built in 1765 which was demolished to make way for Regent's Bridge. The present church has cast iron columns supporting a U-plan gallery. The front exterior is most impressive comprising a recessed central curtain with a 3-bay plastered and entablatured central panel at first floor level. Within the building is a memorial tablet which commemorates the Rev George Scott (1804-74), a former minister between 1872-74, who was appointed a Wesleyan Methodist missionary to Stockholm. His influence became well known and resulted in the establishment of Methodism in Sweden.

The oldest Methodist chapel still in use in Scotland, dating from 1764, is at Dunbar (B16), now a quiet seaside town and former fishing port in East Lothian. It has a rugged coastline of red sandstone and was later the birthplace in 1838 of John Muir, the renowned naturalist and conservationist. He became known as 'the father of American national parks'. Both John and Charles Wesley were trustees of Dunbar Chapel in Victoria Street and

John preached there on 21 occasions. He described it in his Journal as 'the cheerfullest preaching house in the kingdom'. It is a building with much atmosphere and contains stained glass and an ornate oak pulpit originally from St Giles' Cathedral, Edinburgh. If one follows the coastline northwards from Dunbar to North Berwick, an impressive sight out at sea is the Bass Rock massif, now a bird sanctuary for gannets. John Wesley is said to have climbed the Rock to honour the memory of Covenanters who were once held prisoner there.

Wesley's second visit to Scotland in 1753 included Glasgow (B13), and he records in his Journal that 'upwards of one thousand people stayed with all willingness to hear my message' despite a downpour of rain. He later preached in the local prison. Glasgow's first Methodist class leader was Dr John Gillies, minister of the College Kirk, Blackfriars, where Wesley preached as well as in the High Street and town hospital. Dr Gillies also provided him with a movable canvas pulpit for use at outdoor services. He was also the first Church of Scotland minister to introduce Methodist-style singing in his church services. In Glasgow, Wesley considered the cathedral to be 'more lofty than at Canterbury.'

In 1761 John Wesley ventured further north on his fifth Scottish journey which included Dundee (B11) (where, twenty years later, John noted the many improvements which had taken place to properties and gardens within the town – but little in religious matters), Montrose (B8) – where he preached on the Green, Stonehaven (B6) and in Aberdeen (B5), where Methodism had already been established. It was here that he preached to vast crowds at the Town Hall, Marischal College and the King's College Kirk of the University. By the time he left, the Methodist society in Aberdeen had grown to ninety members. On a later occasion, John presented a preaching chair to the congregation at the Methodist chapel (Aberdeen Methodist Church). His return journey was via Glamis (B9) where he saw the ancient castle which has been in the possession of the Lyon family since 1372. It was later to be the childhood home of the late Queen Elizabeth the Queen Mother, and birthplace of her late daughter, Princess Margaret, in 1930. Wesley continued his journey south via Edinburgh, Haddington (birthplace of John Knox, spiritual leader and founder of the Reformation in Scotland in the 16th century) and Dunbar where he preached on 12 and 13 May.

He was in the north-east of Scotland again in 1764, visiting Dundee, Aberdeen and Monymusk, 19 miles (30 km) north, where his colleague Sir Archibald Grant, built a model village for his workers. Wesley then headed across the county of Moray to Elgin (B3) where he saw the extensive ruins of the Cathedral which was desecrated during the Reformation. It was not until his seventh journey that he visited Banff (B4) in stormy weather on his way to Nairn (B2), later crossing the fast-flowing River Spey en route to Inverness. The Methodist society in Inverness (B1) owes its origin to Christopher Hopper, the itinerant preacher and friend of Wesley. John's first visit to the town was in June 1764 when he preached in the High Church at five thirty in the late afternoon. It was six years before his next visit when he preached at the same venue, at Dunbar's Hospital, and also nearby Fort George. His next appearance in Inverness was not until 1779, by which time he found a flourishing society of about sixty members. Methodism first took root in the town around the area of Academy Street.

In the following year Wesley travelled to Portpatrick (B29) on his way to join the ferry to Ireland then, in 1770, northwards from Edinburgh to Dalwhinnie (B7), accompanied by John Helton, another of his preachers. Here Wesley was snowed up in 'the dearest inn I have met in north Britain'. On reaching Inverness again John preached four times. Although he visited the town on four occasions it was only his preachers who actually ventured further into other areas of northern Scotland and to the Outer Hebrides. On the return journey Wesley called in at Arbroath to visit the local Methodist society.

He visited Arbroath (B10) a total of fifteen times on nine of his journeys. Methodism first arrived in the person of Thomas Cherry, a newly appointed minister to Dundee. Cherry first preached in Abbey Pend to a small group of people, among whom was Mr James Millar, a mason, who invited him to hold further meetings in his workshop. Wesley paid his first visit in 1770 and discovered an enthusiastic group of people. Before he left, John gave instructions for the building of a meeting house in Arbroath to be of his favourite octagonal design. It was given the name 'Totum Kirkie' (a totum being an eight-sided spinning toy). At the same time a single storey cottage was built for the minister and stabling for horses, gardens and a supply of water were provided. In 1772, on his second visit, Wesley opening the new buildings. The chapel, though much altered, was later renamed St John's Methodist Church while the old manse was named Wesley House in the early 20th century.

On his visit in 1772, Wesley was made a Freeman of the City of Perth (B12) and he preached at various places including the South Inch, Watergate and Tolbooth. To the north-east of Perth is Scone Palace, the home of Wesley's friend, William Murray (later first Earl of Mansfield) who had been a school friend of his brother, Charles, at Westminster School in London. Scone was the ancient coronation site of Scottish kings.

John Wesley must have noticed the great contrast between the dirt and squalor of many of the Scottish towns in the 18th century compared with the magnificent scenery of the open countryside, lochs and lofty mountains, especially as he travelled north into the Highlands. It could not have failed to please or invigorate him.

*St John's Church, Arbroath*

# CHAPTER 16

# The North-West, Cumbria and Isle of Man

WESLEY'S JOURNEYS TO SCOTLAND usually meant travelling up the west coast of England and back via the east, or the route in reverse. It would be the norm to travel via the east coast in winter months as the terrain of Cumbria, and of some parts of the north-west, is more mountainous and the likelihood of inclement weather greater – whether riding on horseback or by carriage it would have proved treacherous.

Manchester (C19) was Wesley's major centre in the north-west. It was already at the heart of a growing conurbation of Lancashire towns caught up in the textile industry supplemented by wool from Pennine sheep and mountains of the Lake District. The Industrial Revolution was just beginning to take hold in Wesley's day and people flocked to the expanding northern towns to seek employment in the newly mechanised industries. It was also a time of forced child labour and employment of women in long and unsociable hours, dreadful working conditions and hard toil for little reward. Mill and landowners worked their employees to the limit giving little consideration for their health or social welfare. Misery and depression amongst the workers were often obliterated for a few hours by heavy drinking. Drunkenness, in turn, led to family poverty as hard-earned wages were frittered away on liquor, often causing shortages of food and under-nourishment for workers' starving families. Large families and a high infant mortality rate were the norm. It was a situation into which Methodism began to make substantial inroads.

Wesley made 24 visits to Stockport which, though in Cheshire, is now considered part of the Manchester conurbation. A small chapel was erected in Hillgate, which was rebuilt in 1784. In 1790 Wesley preached in Altrincham at a church belonging to St Margaret's parish, and also at a Moravian chapel in Audenshaw. In the centre of Manchester is St Anne's Parish Church, dating from 1709-12, and now an elegant part of the city's central shopping area. The church overlooks St Anne's Square and was once a building in which Wesley was given permission to preach. It was 1733 when he first arrived in Manchester to see his friend and former Oxford Methodist, John Clayton. Clayton had been appointed curate of Trinity Church, Salford (where Wesley was also allowed to preach). At the time John discussed with his colleague the question as to whether he should succeed his father at Epworth. After some deliberation he decided against it. The two friends met again after John's return from Georgia.

The first Methodist preaching house in Manchester was built in Birchin Lane, but has long since disappeared. John Wesley preached there on Easter Day, 1751. The building became the nerve centre for the local Methodist fraternity until a later chapel was opened in Oldham Street thirty years later. (This was eventually demolished and the present Methodist Central Hall built on the same site). John also preached in Manchester Cathedral when John Clayton became its chaplain and where the first sermons in this area on Methodist themes were preached. It is a 15th century structure in Perpendicular Gothic style and was given cathedral status in 1847. A tower was added in 1868 but its chief glory is the early 16th century carved woodwork, especially the canopied choir stalls. Whilst in the vicinity Wesley also visited the ancient Chetham Hospital and Library which stands opposite the Cathedral.

Humphrey Chetham (1580-1653) was one of Manchester's benefactors who left funds to found a school for the poor and for a public library. The school, Chetham's Hospital, was opened in 1656 and has since become famous as Chetham's School of Music, which develops the talents of musically gifted young people. Chetham's Library was the first free library in Europe and contains manuscripts and books from the 16th century.

Manchester also houses the John Rylands University of Manchester Library in Deansgate, which holds the Methodist Archives and Research Centre, being the main repository of the Connexional records of the British Methodist Church. It also holds one of the world's richest collections of Evangelical Christian material. As a building it is an architectural gem and, though built in Victorian times, gives one the impression that you are entering one of England's smaller cathedrals with sweeping Gothic arches, stone pillars, and stained glass windows. It has an atmosphere of tranquility common to major churches.

A regular calling place was Warrington (c18) which Wesley visited on twenty occasions. On 15 April 1755 he preached at six in the morning 'to a large and serious congregation'. His final visit was on 7 April 1790 when, as an old man of 87, he had to be supported by two others as he stood in the pulpit to preach, his voice much weakened. This chapel was in Bank Street but he also preached at another in the former Balham Lane.

By and large the growth of Methodism in the north-west had been mainly confined to Manchester until the 1760s when it started to expand into surrounding towns and villages by way of a network of local preachers. In particular, the work began to spread into Liverpool and the area around the River Mersey. The development of industry and the opening up of trade with America and the West Indies transformed Liverpool into a prosperous maritime city. It was also the main packet port between England and Ireland with the consequence that there was a substantial growth in the number of Irish immigrants. Wesley described Liverpool as 'one of the neatest, best-built towns I have seen in England. I think it is fully twice as large as Chester; most of the streets are quite straight.'

Over recent years Merseyside has become synonymous with the entertainment business, having produced a number of well-known actors, comedians and a plethora of musical groups – as epitomised by The Beatles – who brought international fame to the city. There is both a large Anglican cathedral and a Roman Catholic one, the contemporary and unusual design of the latter having given rise to its nickname of 'Paddy's Wigwam'. The two sites are connected by the appropriately-named Hope Street.

The main Methodist chapel in Liverpool (C17) was in Pitt Street, sadly demolished in 1905, where in 1765 Wesley was shown three new galleries which had been added. The other chapel was at Mount Pleasant in the town centre. This was also closed in 1905, the second of only two which had survived from Wesley's day. On a later visit to Liverpool in April 1777 Wesley states in his Journal that 'many large ships are now laid up in the docks, which had been employed for many years in buying or stealing poor Africans, and selling them in America for slaves. The men butchers have now nothing to do at this laudable occupation. Since the American war broke out, there is no demand for human cattle. So the men of Africa, as well as Europe, may enjoy their native liberty.' This change in affairs would have gladdened his heart.

There were visits to many of the smaller Lancashire towns such as Wigan (for years proverbially known as 'wicked Wigan'), Darwen, St Helen's, Bury (where he visited Mr. Peel's calico works – one of his descendants was Sir Robert Peel, twice British Prime Minister and founder of the London Metropolitan Police), Bolton, Rochdale and others. In Oldham he preached in the Manchester Street Chapel on 5 April 1782. Wesley also visited Rossendale on nine occasions, the first being in 1747. The first chapel there was at Mount Pleasant, Bacup (C15), built in 1761, where John recorded in his Journal 'about noon I preached at Bacup, a village in Rossendale. The new preaching house is large, but not large enough to contain the congregation'. Two more chapels were to follow. A marble tablet now marks the site of the first Methodist chapel and sited at No.18 Lanehead Lane.

Preston's first Methodist meeting place (C16) started in an upper room of the Old Dog Inn at 133 Church Street which stands a few yards below St John's Parish Church. Sir Richard Arkwright, inventor of the spinning frame, was born in Preston in 1732. It was an invention which brought much trade to the town through its cotton-spinning industry. Preston is an ancient town and was the second oldest borough in England, having been represented in Parliament since the 13th century.

Both John Wesley and George Whitefield preached at the end of the market place from the exterior of a former playhouse in the small Cumbrian town of Kendal (C3). It lies at the foot of softly rounded fells south of the Lake District and is a place famous for its mint cake (regularly used by climbers and explorers for sustenance). Kendal became known as 'the auld grey town' because of its many fine old houses and other buildings of grey limestone. The 14th century ruined castle was once the home of Catherine Parr, the last wife of Henry VIII and the only one to survive him.

In Penrith (B26), a preaching room in Crown Terrace Yard, off King Street, was used by John Wesley. This route would have given him access along the Eden valley to tracks which led across the Northern Dales. After skirting Morecambe Bay and Kent's Bank towards the Furness area, John Wesley was not very impressed with Ulverston. He did not draw the crowd he was expecting. The town later came to prominence as the birthplace of Hollywood film comedian Stan Laurel of the famous Laurel and Hardy partnership. A Laurel and Hardy Museum has been established there and contains memorabilia of the famous pair.

Travelling deeper into the Lake District, Wesley stayed at the 17th century Salutation Inn in Ambleside (C2) and preached from its steps. He occasionally stayed overnight on his way over the mountains to Whitehaven and the Cumbrian coastal towns via Wrynose and Hardknott Pass. Whitehaven (C1) developed in the 12th century as the port of nearby St Bees Priory. During the 18th century it became a coal mining centre and the town was expanded by the Lowther family to cater for a growing population. As well as exporting coal it also imported tobacco from the Americas through its busy harbour. Wesley preached at St Nicholas Church and in Michael Street Chapel, both since rebuilt, and also in the market place. It was also at Whitehaven that his brother Charles came to dissuade him from marrying Grace Murray. As well as preaching to a thriving Methodist society in the town, John used the port to sail to and from the Isle of Man and Ireland.

In Northern Lakeland the town of Keswick has, over the years, remained a centre for Christian pilgrimage and witness (as in the annual Keswick Convention). Keswick was on one of Wesley's regular routes, and he met with a thriving Methodist community in the town. He also made many visits to Cockermouth (B28), birthplace of poet William Wordsworth on 7 April 1770 in a handsome house – open to the public – in the tree-lined Main Street.

In Carlisle (B27), Wesley met a man who had been blind since the age of four. On one occasion the man was locked in the organ loft of the local parish church and had felt every part of the organ. Afterwards he made an organ for himself, which, according to witnesses, was a very good one. He then taught himself to play psalms, anthems, voluntaries and anything he heard with great accuracy. John Wesley preached in Carlisle several times, often at the Old Town Hall in Greenmarket. It has two curved staircases with iron balustrades leading to its first floor main entrance – a good vantage point for Wesley to preach from. The building is now an excellent Visitor and Tourist Information Centre.

John Wesley made two visits to the Isle of Man. During the course of these trips John managed to cover most of the island and met many of his sympathisers. On his first visit in May 1777 he travelled overnight by boat from Whitehaven and landed at Douglas at eight in the morning. On arriving, he preached at the market place in a building to the rear of Victoria Street Church. On first sight of the town he felt it reminded him very much of Newlyn in Cornwall both in situation and the architectural style of its buildings. He was then taken by chaise to Castletown in the southern part of the island where he preached near Castle Rushen at six in the evening. Once again, he was not allowed by a local bishop to preach in the parish church. The chair on which Wesley stood to address his congregations is still kept as an exhibit in the ancient castle. John stayed the night at a house in Arbury Street, Castletown, and, next morning, set off up the western coast of the island to the small town of Peel where he preached from a hillside. He then journeyed towards the centre of the island in order to return to Douglas for his return passage to Whitehaven.' John's second visit to the Isle of Man in May 1781 was of slightly longer duration. From Douglas he again travelled to Castletown and Peel (where on the seashore he addressed the largest congregation of his visit). He travelled on towards Ballaugh where the preaching house proved too small to contain everyone. On another day he took a trail from Ramsay, where he once preached in the old square at the end of Church Street. Wesley continued through the wooded area of Sulby – with its small Wesleyan chapel in the valley – to Kirkmichael to visit the grave of Bishop Wilson and passed 'Bishopcourt' where Wilson once lived. John again preached in Peel to a large crowd where he admired the singers and met them after the service. On the following day he arranged a meeting with his twenty-two local preachers from the island and rode over to Dawby in the afternoon to preach to another hearty congregation. John Wesley was very satisfied with the state of Methodism as he found it on the Isle of Man and returned to the English mainland to continue his journeys.

# CHAPTER 17

# Wales and The Marches

ONE OF THE PROBLEMS which John Wesley encountered in Wales was his lack of knowledge of the Welsh language. In many parts of the country, especially the north, locals spoke no other tongue than Welsh and it often made communication difficult for outsiders. John often travelled through Wales on his way to Ireland.

Wesley received a pressing invitation to visit Wales and it was on the green of the small village at the foot of Devauden Hill, north of Chepstow, that he preached his first sermon in the Principality on 15 October 1739. He travelled on to Abergavenny where he addressed about a thousand people in the early evening. Over the next three days he visited Pontypool, Newport and Cardiff. In Newport Parish Church (E27), on the morning of 19 October, John had problems with an old man who cursed and swore throughout his sermon as well as threatening him with a large stone. That evening he preached in the Shire Hall in Cardiff (E28) on 'The Beatitudes' with a number of the local gentry present. On other occasions John preached in the grounds of ancient Cardiff Castle and at nearby Llandaff Cathedral. Legend has it that the saint Dyfrig who crowned Arthur as King of Britain is buried in the cathedral. In more modern times, a large 20th century sculpture of Christ in Majesty by Jacob Epstein has dominated the centre of the nave within the ancient building. In reality it conceals the organ pipes.

## *Welsh Calvinistic Methodists – Howell Harris*

The Principality had been influenced by Puritan preachers in the 17th century and early signs of a religious Revival began to emerge in 1714 when a minister named Griffith Jones started to preach in the open air. These flames were fanned a few years later when another clergyman, Daniel Rowland, and a layman named Howell Harris started to play leading roles in a sect which became known as the Welsh Calvinistic Methodists (now the Presbyterian Church of Wales) which had links with George Whitefield. Harris was converted in 1735 at St Gwendoline's Church, Talgarth. After that experience he began a life of complete dedication to God. He started to hold small gatherings at his mother's cottage at Trefeca (E30), just below the Black Mountains near Brecon, and soon became an itinerant preacher. Although Harris was never ordained as a minister and always remained a lay preacher and member of the Church of England, through his influence and spiritual work he became known as the founder of Welsh Calvinistic Methodism. With the help of the Countess of Huntingdon they founded a community in 1752 at Trefeca. By 1842 a college had also been opened to train new preachers. Displays at Coleg Trefeca show aspects of the life of Howell Harris and the site is open to the public on weekdays by appointment.

John Wesley, John Fletcher and George Whitefield each visited Trefeca and lodged in the nearby Farmhouse. As Wesley describes it, 'Howell Harris's house is one of the most elegant places which I have seen in Wales.'

Unlike many other members of the Welsh Methodist movement, Howell Harris was committed to union between Wesleyans, Moravians, and the various factions within the Church of England. However, differences of expression between Harris and Daniel Rowlands led to a confrontation at Llanidloes in 1751 and a subsequent split in the Methodist Connexion.

\* \* \*

There are many locations in South Wales where Wesley preached. Wenvoe near Cardiff was a regular calling place where one of his Oxford colleagues, John Hodges, was rector. Wesley often stayed with him and preached in the 13th century church of St Mary's. Hodges occasionally went along with his friend to some of the meetings and was later buried in the local churchyard. John Wesley also preached in Porthkerry Church, close to the coast near Barry Island and his brother Charles also visited the site.

Between Barry and Llantwit Major is the 13th century Fonmon Castle (E29) where John often preached and stayed as a guest of the widowed Mrs Robert Jones. It was bought in 1656 by Colonel Philip Jones during the English Civil War and Oliver Cromwell had been an earlier visitor. The Castle is still occupied by one of Colonel Jones' direct descendants. A number of letters written by the Wesley brothers are kept in the building, some of which refer to the education of Mrs Jones' only son, Robert, at Kingswood School from where he absconded. The Castle is open to the public during summer months on Tuesday and Wednesday. Cowbridge was on Wesley's route in a westerly direction where he stopped off to address the crowds in the Market Hall.

Swansea (E31), Llanelli and Llandefaelog were other places visited by Wesley. He called at Llanelli on eight occasions and preached in both the Parish Church and the churchyard. On his final visit he was given news that a Methodist chapel was about to be built. Whilst in Llanelli the visitor should try and make a point of calling at Parc Howard Mansion, situated a little way out of the town. It is now an art gallery and museum, surrounded by pleasant lawns and gardens, and houses a large collection of local pottery including Wesleyana. On occasions, Wesley also travelled to the beautiful Gower peninsula with its sweeping sandy bays and downlands covered in gorse. In the tiny hamlet of Oxwich by its picturesque bay and rugged coastline is a thatched cottage where he once stayed as guest of John Clarke.

On later occasions John ventured into Pembrokeshire and made fourteen visits to the area. Although the vicar of St Mary's Church in Pembroke invited him to preach in the building, the local mayor objected. It was during visits to the town that John lodged in a room to the rear of the York Tavern. He also preached at other places in the area including Monktown Church, the former St Daniel's Church, and also in the main street. In the same county Wesley preached in Tenby (E32) at the town cross and, on his visit in August 1784, states that 'two thirds of the ancient town are either in ruins or vanished away'. He later visited St David's, the smallest city in Britain, but was dismayed by the town and the crumbling state of its cathedral.

Wesley always considered his Haverfordwest Circuit (E33) as the most important in Wales. It is situated between South and Central Wales, and Methodism had a strong following in the region. During overnight stays John usually lodged with the sheriff, Mr Green, at No. 24 Bridge Street. Wesley often preached and baptized in the local Methodist chapel approached via Chapel Lane, and occasionally addressed crowds in Queen Square. It was on his last visit to Haverfordwest and, indeed, to Wales, in August 1790 that John preached from a horse block outside the Blue Boar hostelry. This once stood near to the fish market.

On 14 July 1777, John Wesley preached at the small seaside town of Newport in Cardigan Bay and the following day was taken by chaise to Cardigan where he spoke to a large crowd – including a number of clergymen.

Even by 1750 the small town of Holywell in North Wales was included on a 'Circuit Plan' of preacher John Bennet (who married Grace Murray) and by 1762 a Methodist society had also been established in Mold. Holywell had long been a place of pilgrimage through St Winifred's Well and shrine. According to legend, Winifred refused an offer of marriage by a Welsh prince who was so angered that he cut off her head. The story goes that the head rolled away to rest at a spot from whence a spring burst from the ground. When St Beuno, her uncle, saw this he joined the head to the body – and they were instantly reunited! In the 15th century an enshrined well was built over the holy spring which soon became a place of pilgrimage. In Mold, John Wesley preached in a field known as Coetiau Moch, situated off Clay Lane, and close to the Parish Church. This land has since been built upon. A few miles south-west of Mold is the historic town of Denbigh where, in Factory Place, is Capel Pendref, the first Wesleyan Methodist chapel to be built where the Welsh language was used. It was opened in 1802.

Wesley's excursions into North Wales usually started from Chester (c30) from where he often followed an old coach road which led by way of St Asaph (c31) and Bettws-yn-Rhos. (St Asaph has the smallest cathedral in Wales which replaced a simple Celtic sanctuary of St Kentigern.) Wesley preached in Wrexham in 1871 where he wrote that 'a flame was kindled both in Chester and Wrexham which, I trust, will not soon be put out'. On some occasions, John travelled to Wales via Shrewsbury, Llangollen and Llanrwst. Both routes led to the ancient town of Conway (c32). In describing Conway Castle, Wesley states it is 'the noblest ruin I ever saw. An arm of the sea runs round two sides of the hill on which the castle stands – once the delight of kings, now overgrown with thorns, and inhabited by doleful birds only.' On reaching Penmaen-Mawr he described the local scenery as such – 'a ragged cliff hangs over one's head, as if it would fall any moment'. Former Prime Minister William Gladstone was a regular visitor to the area and loved tramping the hills above the town. Continuing along the North Wales coast Wesley was obviously impressed by the range of mountains, valleys and cornfields on one side with the prospect of the sea on the other. He was also taken with the large and handsome 14th century cathedral at Bangor, burial places of some of the Welsh bishops and princes, whose foundation is older than that at Canterbury.

Wesley used a ferry to cross the Menai Straits to the Island of Anglesey, a place he visited on sixteen occasions. It was usually

*Conway Castle*

when travelling to catch the ferry from Holyhead to Ireland. Sometimes he preached in the town of Holyhead (C34) and other parts of the island though, again, the drawback was his lack of knowledge of the Welsh language. This meant he always had to have an interpreter accompany him on such visits. Edward Philips, rector of Maesmynis Church, near Builth, where Wesley often preached, sometimes accompanied him in this capacity, even as far as Caernarvon (C33) where he addressed members of the society and others.

Sometimes John travelled into Wales over the mountains through the Welsh Marches – a name given to the borderland country between England and Wales. This comprises parts of the counties of Gloucester, Hereford, Worcester, Shropshire and Cheshire.

Gloucester (E25) was a regular calling place for John especially in his early days as an itinerant preacher with George Whitefield, who originated from the city. Like Whitefield, Wesley occasionally preached in the town hall. The nearby Forest of Dean covers part of Gloucestershire and well worth a visit is the Dean Heritage Museum (E26) at Soudley near Cinderford. Here stands Zion Chapel which was founded by the Bible Christians in 1846, with a school room added later. The site is open to the public. Also in the same county is Stroud (E24) which has the oldest surviving Methodist octagonal chapel on Chapel Street, built 1762, and now used by the Salvation Army. There is also a plaque in the Shambles area of Stroud which commemorates Wesley's preaching in the town.

On his trips into Herefordshire John occasionally rode by way of the Malvern Hills which he describes as 'offering one of the finest prospects in the kingdom'. Much later the composer Sir Edward Elgar – who lived in the area – would have agreed. The ancient market town of Ledbury was the first place he reached on his route to Ross-on-Wye and Hay-on-Wye (the latter having become famous over recent years as England's 'second hand books' capital). From there, he travelled onwards to Monmouth to preach and then into South Wales.

Every year John Wesley paid a visit to Worcestershire and the valley of the River Severn. He first preached in the county at the attractive town of Evesham around 1760. The south side of Pump Street in Worcester (E35) has been a hub of Methodist tradition for over 200 years during which five different churches have graced the same site. Wesley often visited the first Wesleyan chapel in New Street, built 1772, and on 24 March 1784 also preached to a crowded congregation in the now-ruined St Andrew's Parish Church (only the church tower and slender spire have survived Second World War damage). John always regarded his Worcester society as second only to Bristol as the most exemplary in the country. Of the nearby Severn-side towns, Wesley preached in the delightful centres of Tewkesbury – with its magnificent Abbey dating back to Norman times and containing Romanesque and decorated style of Gothic architecture – Upton-on-Severn and Stourport-on-Severn (E36).

On his first visit to Stourport in 1787 John preached at a temporary meeting place at the rear of a house in New Street. Twelve months later, and again in 1790, he returned to speak in the newly-built chapel just off Parkes' Passage. Shortly afterwards the site was licensed by the Bishop of Worcester as a place of worship for Protestant Dissenters. Alterations were made to the chapel in 1896 when an exquisitely-carved marble and alabaster pulpit was installed. Close by is the lovely Georgian town of Bewdley on the River Severn where on 18 March 1779 Wesley addressed his congregation in the main street. The attractive Methodist chapel was built in 1795 and stands in the High Street opposite the Baptist chapel and a row of terraced houses.

Journeys into mid-Wales were sometimes by the northern route through Mold. At other times John would negotiate on horseback some of the tracks across the Cambrian mountains, through places such as Newtown, Llanidloes, Builth Wells and Llandovery, and head towards the coastal towns of Caernarfon, Porthmadog and Harlech. Wesley's last visit to Wales was in 1789 when he travelled from Shrewsbury to Llangollen, Llanrwst, Conway, and on to Holyhead. He was aged 86 and had completed nearly fifty journeys to different parts of this 'land of song' where many hymns of Charles Wesley have since become part of Wales's traditional repertoire of national music.

# CHAPTER 18

# Ireland

JOHN WESLEY MADE twenty-one visits to Ireland between the years of 1747 and 1789. It was then under British rule. Even so, a British diplomat at the time described Ireland as 'one tangled web of dreadful hates'. He goes on to relate it as 'a corrupt aristocracy, a ferocious commonalty, a distracted Government, a divided people'. It was a country where the Catholic majority were ruled by a Protestant minority. It was therefore possible that the influence or impact of such a person as Wesley might perhaps change peoples' lives and situations for the better.

George Whitefield paid a short visit to Ireland in 1738 on his return from Georgia and was given a good reception by the bishops and their congregations. The first evangelical preaching was actually done by the Moravian, John Cennick, who founded a society in Dublin (D12) and acquired a former Baptist meeting place in Skinner's Alley. Another society was formed in Dublin by Thomas Williams, the first Methodist preacher to visit Ireland. It was he who invited Wesley to Ireland to visit his congregation.

On his first visit to Ireland in 1747 at the age of 44, Wesley was accompanied by preachers John Trembath and William Tucker. (Five years earlier, on 12 April, the first performance of Handel's *Messiah* had been given in Dublin at the Music Hall in Fishamble Street.) They landed on 9 August from a packet boat at St George's Quay on the River Liffey, the journey from Holyhead having taken twenty-six hours. When they arrived in the Irish capital on the Sunday morning the sound of church bells could be heard as they walked towards St Mark's Church to take part in morning worship. That evening Wesley was invited by the curate of St Mary's Church in Mary Street to preach at Evensong. It was therefore in this church that John Wesley preached his first sermon in Ireland. At six the next morning he addressed a congregation on the text 'Repent and believe the Gospel'. (Sadly, only a few remains can be seen of the building where both playwright Richard Brinsley Sheridan and statesman Lord Charlemont were baptized – only the chapter house still stands). In the evening Wesley preached at Marlborough Street Chapel, considered to be the first Methodist place of worship in Ireland but initially built in 1689 as a Lutheran Church. After a meeting with the local Archbishop, Dr Cobbe, it was obvious His Grace had no time for Methodism and its ways. It was not long afterwards that persecution of Methodists began and riots were led by apprentices from the local weaving trade.

During his stay in Dublin, John visited Phoenix Park (a large piece of land to the west of the central area once owned by the Knight Hospitalers of St John of Jerusalem). He later visited other local churches – St James, Christ Church, and often worshipped in St Patrick's Cathedral – and occasionally lodged at No.15 Francis Street. He regularly addressed congregations in a preaching house known as the Whitefriar Street Chapel where, in 1767, he conducted 'the most solemn watch-night service he remembered in Ireland'. Later, a school, ministers' residence, widows' home and bookshop were added to the building. On another occasion he paid his first visit to Trinity College and other sites in the capital such as Dublin Castle. At Trinity College he would have seen the famous Book of Kells, one of the oldest illuminated books in the world, probably produced circa AD 800. It is thought to have been created by the monks of St Columba's monastery on the island of Iona off the west coast of Scotland, and brought to the monastery of Kells in County Meath for safekeeping from Viking raids. In 1653 it was taken to Dublin for protection from the ravages of Cromwell and, in 1661, given to Trinity College. Later, in 1756, Wesley attended worship in the college chapel which undoubtedly would have reminded him of his own chapel at Lincoln College, Oxford.

While in the Dublin area there was an occasion when John preached in the French language to French prisoners stationed at the military barracks at Oxmantown. On his second visit to the city the following year, he lodged at 104 Cork Street where he met his brother, Charles. John preached in Cork Street, Marlborough Street, Ship Street, Skinner's Alley and Newgate Prison. He also addressed a large crowd in the city, mostly Roman Catholic, who gathered to hear him despite the prohibitions of their own clergy. After a short stay in Dublin he moved on to other places including Moate (D10), Philipstown (which he described as 'the most stupid senseless place I have seen in all Ireland') and Tullamore. He eventually arrived in Athlone (D9) where he first witnessed a clear view of the River Shannon. Whilst preaching on Easter Sunday Wesley spotted a local priest attempting to drive away his congregation. There was much anger, eggs were thrown, and the crowd were almost on the point of dismantling the preaching house. Nevertheless, he carried on preaching, undeterred, and made a great impact on his listeners. Later, over one hundred followers accompanied him as he left Athlone for Tullamore on his return route to Dublin.

Grace Murray accompanied Wesley on his Irish tour of 1749 during the time of their courtship, along with William Tucker. After landing John walked into the city of Dublin whilst Grace rode behind in a chaise. During their first week he suffered a swelling of the cheek which proved very painful. His remedy was to treat himself by applying boiled nettles and soon reported that the pain had disappeared. This was followed by the appliance of warm treacle!

During this tour Wesley travelled to Limerick (D15) and preached to about two thousand people at the Mardyke. Afterwards he took a walk by the city walls and attended to prayers in the 12th century St Mary's Cathedral. (The building has a square west tower, parapet with Irish battlements, and a confusion of windows in the south façade. The choir area is noted for its 23 misericordes (carved and usually ornate effigies underneath the hinged seats in a church choir stall giving support to the occupant when standing). At the time John was persuaded to by-pass the city of Cork (D19) due to pending riots and, after visiting Bandon, met with some of the Cork members in Blarney. Violence in Cork led Wesley to publish his appeal for toleration in his address To the Inhabitants of Ireland. In the next year Wesley decided to visit the city to face the music.

Not unexpectedly, his first visit to Cork in 1750 brought a rough reception from the crowd. The rabble marched through the town and burnt an effigy of Wesley near Daunt's Bridge. Fortunately, he was protected by soldiers, many of whom later became Methodists, and they were able to keep the mob at bay and quell the rioting. Wesley rode on to Bandon (D20) where, preaching in the main street, he had to contend with three opponents – a drunken priest, a young man firing a pistol, and a local butcher who tried to attack him by delivering several blows to the head. Next day, undaunted, Wesley preached three times in the town. By 1752 rioting had ceased in Cork and the society was confident enough to start constructing a Chapel in the Marsh (at the corner of the present Henry and Moore Streets), only the second Methodist chapel to be built in Ireland. It had preachers' quarters over the chapel modelled on the Whitefriar Street chapel in Dublin. Consequently, in 1756, Wesley preached in Hammond's Marsh Chapel for the first time, a place to which he often returned. Eventually by 1787 John was accepted in Cork and officially received at the Mansion House by the mayor and guardians of the town.

On Wesley's visit to Ireland in 1752 he was newly married and accompanied by his wife, Molly, the former Mrs Vazeille. He preached in Dublin at five in the morning. At midday he attended the service in St Patrick's Cathedral where he proclaimed he was 'shocked at the careless and indecent [unruly] behaviour of the congregation'. (Jonathan Swift – author of Gulliver's Travels, published in 1726 – had earlier served as Dean between 1713-45 in this, the longest medieval church in Ireland.) From Dublin they travelled to Edenderry, Closeland and Portarlington (D13) where John was taken ill but still managed to address the crowd. By the next day in Mountmellick (D13) he was too hoarse so was compelled to preach indoors. The provincial tour continued to

Tullamore, Coolalough, and Tyrell's Pass and finally reached Limerick, where on 14-15 August, Wesley held his First Irish Conference. Thereafter, these were held annually in various locations whenever Wesley was on a tour of Ireland.

In 1756 John landed at the Howth near Dublin and set out for Cork, preaching in Kilkenny (D16) and Clonmel on his travels. He continued to Limerick, a place where he preached to German Protestant refugees, known as Palatines, who settled in the area. Many became Methodists and from their number came Philip Embury and his cousin, Barbara Heck from Ballingrane, who, with another native of Ireland, Robert Strawbridge, were to take Methodism to New York and Maryland in America. (Wesley met Strawbridge at Terryhoogan in County Leitrim). In 1766 the local Palatine community built a Methodist church in Ballingrane (D17) on a site donated by the Heck family to replace an earlier meeting house. John Wesley visited the village thirteen times between the years 1756-79 and there are some interesting memorial tablets in the chapel, in particular to Embury and Heck. One of the relics on view is a large cow's horn which was sounded to inform local folk that a preacher had arrived. (A memorial window in Donegall Square Methodist Church in Belfast depicts the Embury-Heck link between Irish and American Methodism).

Wesley's tour continued to nearby Adare (D17) where, according to tradition, Wesley preached under an ash tree near the ruins of the Franciscan abbey during one of his ten visits. A stone now marks the spot. Rathaheen was the next place to be visited and then on to preach at Clarecastle and Ennis (D14) where he addressed a large multitude in the Court House before setting off for Galway where accommodation had been secured in a private home. The itinerary for this Irish tour was extended to take in parts of Ulster. The first town they came to was Newry (D5) which he likened to Liverpool in its manner of building. Four days later they arrived in Belfast (D3), then the largest town in Ulster, where there was only one Episcopal church and three Presbyterian meeting houses. John also made an afternoon visit to Carrickfergus where he preached in the session-house. On one occasion he walked to the shores of Lough Neagh and regarded it as 'the most beautiful lake I ever saw' on what he felt was the hottest day he had spent in Ireland. In 1775, writing from Armagh to the Secretary of State for the Colonies, the Earl of Dartmouth, Wesley urged the British government to bring to an end the war with America.

Wesley first visited Lisburn (D3) in County Down in 1756 – a place he was to visit on fourteen occasions – where he made a great impression on Mr and Mrs Hans Cumberland who invited him to stay with them at their small house and bakery in Bow Street. Initially John was pessimistic about a Methodist society in Lisburn but the respect in which Mrs Cumberland was held by the local population ensured there was no opposition to the plan. On one occasion Wesley had a visit from the Rector of Lisburn and his curate and they enjoyed two hours of friendly conversation. In 1765 he addressed a crowd of people in the Linen Hall and also listened to an inspiring sermon in the 17th century Cathedral (the Assembly Rooms now house the Lisburn Museum and Irish Linen Centre which has an extensive display devoted to Northern Ireland's most important craft industry since the 17th century). Later, in 1785 John was invited to preach in the Presbyterian meeting house to a large congregation and on his last visit in 1789 preached in the original Methodist chapel.

On the 1765 tour of Ireland Wesley crossed from Portpatrick (B29) in Scotland and reached Donaghadee. He and accompanying friends set out for Newtownards (D4) and, according to Wesley's Journal, he preached on the Green and 'encouraged the poor, scattered, dejected people'. He also visited Londonderry (D2) on this tour where he preached in another Linen Hall to 'the largest congregation I have seen in the north of Ireland'.

County Sligo was a place John covered in the 1758 tour and, whilst travelling through Jamestown, Carrick-on-Shannon and Boyle (D8), felt it was the best part of Ireland he had seen. Besides preaching in Sligo (D7), Wesley also visited the Dominican Abbey founded in 1252 but destroyed by fire in 1414. The ruins now standing date from subsequent rebuilding. Wesley recorded that 'you can scarce tread unless you will step upon skulls or human bones, which are everywhere scattered up and down'. Waterford (D18) was a regular calling place but when Wesley attempted to reach the town in 1750, the boatman refused to take him and his colleagues across the Graimah Ferry for fear of rioters. In 1760 Wesley conducted a service in the new preaching house which had been opened in Factory Lane. On another occasion John visited Christ Church Cathedral where he was concerned to hear a young clergyman describe Methodists as 'grievous wolves'. Consequently he wrote a pointed reply which was later published in Dublin. Two years on, the same young man was appointed Archdeacon of Waterford but lived to acknowledge the folly of his earlier utterances. John's following increased in the town and, on later occasions, he addressed large crowds in the Court House. Wesley also preached in John Street in 1750 where he was faced with an overdressed vagrant singing risqué songs from the top of a table.

Glass manufacture has taken place in Waterford area since the 17th century and, over recent years, Waterford Crystal has become world famous for its craftsmanship and glass technology.

It was during his visit to Ireland in 1765 that John Wesley was persuaded by a friend to sit for a portrait by a Dublin artist, Robert Hunter. He sat only once for over three and a half hours during which time the artist only completed the face. Wesley thought it a good likeness but friends thought otherwise. In 1778, after preaching in Limavady, Kilrea and Coleraine, he was taken, at his own request, to see the Giant's Causeway (D1), that remarkable basaltic formation of hexagonal pillars ranked as one of the natural wonders of the world.

At the age of 82 Wesley, while on the road to Athenry (D11) in County Galway, was told that a small girl 'had sat up all night, and walked two miles to see him'. John offered her a lift in his carriage and was most surprised to find her 'continually rejoicing in God'. Later, at the age of twelve she was converted and lived a consistent Christian life in Dublin for more than sixty years.

On his next Irish tour two years later, John visited Enniskillen (D6) where the results of his many years of spreading the Gospel were beginning to blossom as indeed they were in many other parts of Ireland. He said of his Enniskillen congregation the 'lions are become lambs'. On his farewell visit to Ireland in 1789 John preached almost one hundred sermons in sixty towns and villages during a nine-week tour. In total, Wesley spent almost six months of his life in Ireland and preached in every county except Kerry. This must have been quite some feat of stamina and determination for someone aged 86. A truly remarkable man! The seeds of Irish Methodism, with the support of his preachers and many societies, had been well and truly sown.

*Giant's Causeway, Co Antrim*

# CHAPTER 19

# Middle England and East Anglia

WESLEY'S JOURNEYS TOOK him almost the length and breadth of the British Isles and he frequently travelled from Cornwall or Bristol to Newcastle-upon-Tyne or Scotland within the space of a few months. It meant he often crossed those counties situated in Middle England which probably led to them receiving a greater share of visits from the great preacher than those places in outlying areas. His third main base was, of course, London, where from the 1740s he returned during winter months. It became a natural start and finishing point for tours of the South and East of England. Let us take a look at some of these counties he often passed through and the events or sites of particular significance.

In 1784 he paid a visit to Nottingham General Hospital and was greatly impressed in the way it was run and, subsequently, preached a charity sermon in nearby Derby to assist hospital funds. He also made later visits when in the Nottingham area. The site of Wesley's first Methodist chapel in Nottingham was the Octagon in Milton Street which has since been covered by the Victoria shopping centre. In 1787 Wesley made a special journey from London to Newark in the same county to open the Guildhall Street Chapel. He also addressed a large crowd in the cobbled market place of this ancient town on the River Trent, dominated by its late 12th century castle. On two other occasions, John encountered rowdy mobs when he preached in the market place at nearby Retford in North Nottinghamshire.

Not far south of Nottingham is Donington Park in the county of Leicestershire. This was once the home of the Countess of Huntingdon, the famous benefactress, with whom Wesley stayed several times between 1742-48. The vast hall was built in the

Gothic style with castellated turrets but has since disappeared. (Donington Park is far better known today as one of the prime motor racing circuits and racing car collections in Britain.) Just a few miles away is the small market town of Ashby-de-la-Zouch where Wesley once preached in the yard of the 14th century Bull's Head Inn situated in Market Street which also claimed Oliver Cromwell as one of its visitors after he captured the local castle for the Parliamentarians during the Civil War. (The castle was the romantic setting for the tournament in Sir Walter Scott's novel *Ivanhoe*.) On 27 May 1783 Wesley addressed congregations at three Leicestershire sites. The first was in Loughborough, now famous for its university and close to the remains of Bradgate House, birthplace of Lady Jane Grey, the tragic nine-day Queen of England; the second was the small town of Mountsorrel; and, finally, the county town of Leicester to which he paid a number of visits over the years. Wesley visited condemned prisoners in Leicester Castle, built by William 1 and overlooking the River Soar, and also chose Castle Green for his first open air preaching engagement. When in Leicester, Wesley sometimes lodged in a cottage opposite St Nicholas Church, the oldest in the city with portions of Anglo Saxon building and Roman stonework. Sadly, the cottage has now gone.

South-west of Coventry is that glorious stretch of undulating countryside known as the Cotswolds which straddles the counties of Warwickshire, Oxfordshire and Gloucestershire. Wesley was a regular visitor and had numerous friends there, and so many places can boast that the great evangelist preached on at least one occasion in their church, market place or on the village green.

The 'honey pot' village of Broadway is one such centre where Wesley preached a funeral sermon in the old parish church of St Eadburga for Robin Griffiths, son of the vicar. The former vicarage where he stayed was opposite the famous Lygon Arms in this beautiful village of honey-coloured Cotswold stone. On 28 August 1767 John preached at Stow-on-the-Wold, once the most prosperous wool town in England, 'to a very dull, quiet congregation'. He had not been invited to preach in the parish church and is thought to have addressed his flock from the base of the medieval cross in the square of this attractive town on the old Roman road Fosse Way. Wesley's visit left its mark and he was followed by other travelling preachers. In Cheltenham there was once a pillared market in the centre of the High Street, opposite the Plough Hotel. It was here that John preached and also on the bowling green of the same inn where he was opposed by the rector of nearby St Mary's church. Wesley often preached in Cheltenham when he was travelling to Worcester to visit his Methodist society.

On the Oxfordshire side of the Cotswolds is the attractive town of Burford (E20) with its wide High Street paved with historic inns, antique shops and town houses. Wesley first preached there to nearly 1,500 people in October 1739, and on four later occasions. The local Methodist society had intended building a preaching house in Sheep Street when they discovered that an outmoded mansion house in the High Street had been put up for sale at a very low price. They bought and refurbished it and domestic offices in the basement were adapted for use as a Sunday School whilst the main body of the building became the chapel. Further along the A40 towards Oxford is the busy town of Witney (E19) where Wesley got caught in a thunderstorm on 16 July 1783. It was a place he visited many times on his way to Bristol and it became an important part of the Methodist movement. While at Witney, John often stayed with friends, the Bolton family, who lived in the nearby manor house at Finstock. Over recent years Witney has become famous for blanket manufacturing, especially in North America. On 24 November 1784, Wesley preached in Banbury (E21), famous for its cross, cakes and nursery rhyme, after receiving a hearty welcome from the Presbyterian minister who offered him the use of his meeting room. Some of the other small towns and villages in Oxfordshire had earlier been visited by John Wesley as an undergraduate at Christ Church and later as Fellow of Lincoln College.

In neighbouring Northamptonshire, Wesley, after travelling all night from London, took breakfast and preached in Towcester on

19 November 1781. The county town of Northampton (E38), best known for its associations with the shoe trade, received 29 visits from the Methodist leader. On one occasion he addressed students of the former Dr Doddridge's Academy in Sheep Street, a building which had once been the town house of the Earl of Halifax. On another occasion, at the small town of Whittlebury, Wesley's servant was taken with a fever 'attended with eruptions all over, as big as pepper-corns.' It turned out to be nettle-rash and he was clear of it within a day. The Methodist church in the town preserves a pulpit used by Wesley and, by tradition, he assisted with building work on the original chapel during his stay.

Perhaps the most famous son produced by Bedfordshire was Nonconformist Baptist scholar and writer, John Bunyan (1628-88), who was imprisoned in Bedford Jail for Dissent. The religious allegory *Pilgrim's Progress*, his best-known work, was written during his imprisonment. On 10 March 1758 John Wesley addressed a large attentive congregation at St Paul's Church in Bedford (F15) before the judge of the local assize court who issued him with an invitation to dine with him after the service. John graciously refused as he had to be on his way to Epworth. On other occasions he preached in an upper room of a 15th century building which formed part of the George Inn on the High Street, and also on St Peter's Green. It was a snowy January day in 1771 when Wesley visited Luton (F16) where he had been offered the pulpit of St Mary's Church. On arrival, he discovered that glass had been removed from the windows on account of a severe frost. It was so cold he might just as well have preached out of doors. On other occasions in Luton he complained of 'drowsy' congregations.

In December 1782 John addressed congregations on consecutive days in both the towns of Huntingdon (F3) and nearby St Neots, where he preached in the former assembly rooms at the north-west corner of the Cross. Travelling into Cambridgeshire, he preached in the small Fenland city of Ely (F5) with its magnificent 11th century Cathedral which he explored. (It is renowned for its Lady Chapel with delicate carved stonework, and the superb octagonal lantern built after the tower collapsed in 1322.) Standing in the shadow of the Cathedral is the former home of England's Lord Protector, Oliver Cromwell. Wesley was not allowed to preach in the Cathedral or other parish churches but in November 1774 he used a nearby house – thought to be that of a local surgeon – situated near the Wheatsheaf Inn (at the corner of West Fen Road and Downham Road). He described it as 'filled with plain loving people'. It seems rather odd that John rarely visited Cambridge (F4) – perhaps it was from the on-going rivalry of England's two premier universities – and there is no record of his preaching there though he was entertained at St John's College in 1731 and dined at The Mitre hostelry.

East Anglia has always been a mainly agricultural region and also, prior to Wesley's day, some of its towns had developed and grown from the prosperity of the woollen industry. Many parish churches were financed and built through monies accrued from this rich trading practice – especially with other European countries as well as other parts of England. Consequently, there were many small towns and villages dotted around the landscape. Like in so many other areas, the Church of England left much to be desired in their pastoral work amongst the workers. As a result, Nonconformist groups began to mushroom and new chapels were erected in Norfolk, Suffolk and Essex. Methodism was no exception.

East Anglia, due to its flatness, must have made for easier travelling for Wesley, especially during winter months. Its capital, Norwich (F8), another fine cathedral city, had a strong Nonconformist following. Both Wesley brothers preached there in 1754 but the society they founded proved rather unruly. For instance, on 30 August 1759 Wesley records 'I preached at the Tabernacle in Norwich to a large, rude, noisy congregation'. (This was in the same year as the British victory over the French and the capture of Quebec in Canada. George II died in 1760 and was succeeded by his grandson as George III.) Later, in 1781, John Wesley preached at Bear Street, Norwich, to 'a large congregation, most of whom had never seen my face before'. Sadly, none of the early Wesleyan chapels survive. He visited King's Lynn (F6) several times, where he founded a society, and also Great Walsingham (F7) in the north of the county. Walsingham had for hundreds of years been a place of pilgrimage and Wesley visited the remains of its abbey in 1781. The village later became the head of a Wesleyan circuit and its chapel of 1793-94 in the High Street is the oldest in East Anglia. Wesley's first visit to Great Yarmouth (F9) was in 1761, when he found it to be a 'wicked seaport'. By 1783 he had opened a new Methodist preaching house at No. 8 Row, since swept away by redevelopment though its pulpit has survived and is kept at Lowestoft Road Methodist Church in nearby Gorleston across the River Yare.

Further down the east coast is the port of Lowestoft (F10) where Wesley preached a number of times and found the society 'affectionate and dependable'. On one occasion in November 1776 he was accompanied by John Fletcher when he opened the new preaching house in High Street, since replaced. On 20

October 1790, then an old man of 87, John preached one of his last sermons in the 13th century parish church of Diss (F11), with the approval of the new Bishop of Norwich, Dr Horne.

Wesley visited historic Bury St Edmunds (F12) on seventeen occasions between 1755-90, always preaching in the open air or in individual houses. It was not until after his death that the first Wesleyan chapel was built in St Mary's Square. The first Methodist place of worship to be built in Suffolk was at Lakenheath and Wesley first went there at the invitation of John Evans. He was a local man, who built a chapel in 1757 and bequeathed it to the Methodists. It was replaced by the present church in 1835 and incorporates an inscribed stone from the original building.

Wesley was fond of looking over old buildings and in Colchester (F13), Britain's oldest recorded town, he enjoyed a tour of William the Conqueror's impressive 11th century castle. It has the largest surviving Norman keep ever built. On his first visit in 1758 and at later dates he preached on St John's Green and also on many occasions in the twelve-sided preaching house, built 1759, in Maidenburgh Street. Francis Asbury was stationed there in 1768-69. A plaque commemorating this original chapel is now on the wall of the present Castle Methodist Church in the same street. The original pulpit used by Wesley and Asbury is preserved within the church.

Despite his age, Wesley still set off on another tour in 1790, his last complete year. Between the months of February and October he travelled across Britain taking in Aberdeen and Glasgow, Newcastle-upon-Tyne, Bristol, Haverfordwest, Manchester, York, Hull and many other places along the way. He returned, as usual, to London.

# CHAPTER 20

# Home Counties and the South

DURING THE LAST eleven years of his life, John Wesley's London residence was the town house in City Road adjacent to Wesley's Chapel. It was to act as his home whenever he was not away on his travels. During the winter he took on more local work both in the adjacent City Road Chapel and in other London parishes, and made short journeys to those areas surrounding London described as the Home Counties and Southern England. He had of course travelled to many of these places previously and already established many thriving Methodist communities.

Buckinghamshire is quite close to Oxford and John regularly preached in some of its villages and small towns during his curacy days at university. However, this was prior to adopting his radical open air preaching and, in later years, Wesley was to find that he was not allowed to use those same parish churches to deliver his message. He preached in High Wycombe (E17) on numerous occasions. In January 1765, one of his congregation was the 32 year-old Hannah Ball. She was so moved by Wesley's sermon that, shortly afterwards, she started to correspond with him on a regular basis and they became firm friends. Hannah lived in High Wycombe for most of her life and became a staunch worker for Methodism. She is generally attributed to be the pioneer of the first Sunday School in the country in 1769 (an accolade wrongly attributed to Robert Raikes who founded his first Sunday School in Gloucester in 1780) and also the main inspiration for a new preaching house in the town which was opened by Wesley on 11 November 1779. Hannah Ball was greatly revered throughout Methodism and died on 16 August 1792 aged 58. She is buried in the graveyard of the 13th century church of St Peter and St Paul at Stokenchurch in the same county. Wesley also preached at

Stony Stratford, now part of Milton Keynes, to a 'large and attentive congregation' on 27 October 1777. Earlier he spoke in the market square and in a barn belonging to the Talbot Inn at 81-83 High Street which had been rented to the Methodists.

Essex was a county more accessible from London and occasionally Wesley took the coastal route through Tilbury (the scene of Elizabeth I's famous morale-boosting speech to her troops preparing to face the Spanish Armada in 1588) to places such as Leigh-on-Sea. He rode there from London in December 1748 in treacherous winter weather to preach at this old fishing village where cockle boats can still be seen unloading their daily catch. Maldon lay on another route where the Methodists' first preaching room was in an old building of Roman origin known as 'Cat's Castle' after a former occupant who lived there with twenty-one cats. At a later date Wesley opened a chapel, the site of which is occupied by Nos. 118-120 High Street.

Hertfordshire was a regular route as the Great North Road from London to Edinburgh passed through the county. In 1786 Wesley called to see Hatfield House (F17), built by Robert Cecil, 1st Earl of Salisbury and Chief Minister to King James I, in 1611. In the extensive and beautiful gardens is the surviving wing of the Royal Palace of Hatfield (circa 1497) where Elizabeth I spent much of her childhood and where she first learned she had become Queen in 1558 at the age of twenty-five. A few miles away in Hockerill, Bishop's Stortford (F14), Wesley described his lodging place, the Red Lion Inn, as 'the dearest I was ever at'.

In the town of Hertford, Wesley addressed two groups of pupils from poor homes at a local school. He first spoke to the girls and most of them burst into tears until he started to pray. In the boys' class his reception was very different and Wesley was greeted with mirth. He continued his lecture on the theme 'and set before them the terrors of the Lord' and this had a profound effect upon the majority. John had never challenged young people in such a moving manner before or to such a good response. On 2 August 1770 Wesley met up in St Albans with friends from London and they all took a walk into the Abbey. In his Journal he describes it as 'one of the most ancient buildings in the kingdom and one of the largest, being longer than Westminster Abbey'. The magnificent building with the longest nave in the world is named after Alban, the Roman citizen of Verulamium who became the first Christian martyr in Britain.

Places connected with John Wesley within the London area north of the River Thames include St Ethelburga's parish church in Bishopsgate where John Wesley preached on 20 February 1785. In the same street is St Helen's Parish Church which has a fine Jacobean pulpit from which both Wesleys preached and, indeed, from where George Whitefield delivered his first sermon. There was the Church of the Holy Sepulchre, the largest of the City of London churches, situated on Holborn Viaduct, where Wesley did not preach until he was seventy-five. In addition, was St Clement Danes in the Strand where John preached to 'an immense congregation'. A mile or two away in the bustling district of Islington is St Mary's Parish Church on Upper Street where, in 1739, Wesley held one of his earliest conferences of Methodist leaders. Eastwards, the area of Bow in the traditional East End of London was still a small community by the River Lea when John Wesley preached there. Just south of Bow is Poplar where Wesley opened a Methodist chapel in Hale Street in 1772.

South of the Thames is Wandsworth where the first Methodist chapel was built in the High Street in 1772. Earlier, John preached at the home of Nathaniel Gilbert, a former West Indian planter and, at the same time, baptized two of his slaves. Up river is the charming suburb of Hampton Court (F18) with its famous Palace built originally by Cardinal Wolsey in the 16th century but seized by Henry VIII in 1526. John Wesley visited the site on two occasions and was extremely impressed with the building but for one aspect. The nude figures appeared to him as 'shockingly immodest and shockingly absurd, offending against common sense as well as against modesty!'

Moving towards Kent is St Mary's Parish Church at Bexley where the Reverend Henry Piers, a close friends of the Wesleys, was vicar. He regularly allowed the brothers to use his pulpit and invited them to stay at the former vicarage (now St Mary's Old People's Home) in Vicarage Lane. Nearby was Blendon Hall, home of Charles Delamotte, one of Wesley's companions when he went to Georgia. John called on this family on his return to England and was made most welcome. Sadly, only the gatehouse of the hall survives at the junction of The Drive and Blendon Road. A mile south of Farningham along the A225 is the picture-postcard village of Eynsford (F19), with timbered houses and a narrow stone bridge from which Wesley is reputed to have preached. About four miles away (6 km) is the rather remote village of Shoreham where the Reverend Vincent Perronet was vicar for almost fifty years and became one of Wesley's most enthusiastic supporters. Johnl visited him annually and their long relationship is commemorated in the parish church. It became Wesley's base for travelling southwards and, for some considerable time, the Sussex circuit was based at this particular Shoreham in Kent.

Sevenoaks is the next main town. Both the Wesleys were confronted with strong opposition when they first preached near Sevenoaks School in 1746. According to tradition, a local blacksmith grabbed hold of one of the rioters and took him back to his forge (now part of the Royal Oak hostelry in the High Street) where he hung him by the belt from one of the hooks until the sermon was ended. The house where John Wesley stayed was No. 20 London Road (now Williamson's butchers shop). To the east of the town is Knole (National Trust), one of the great treasure houses of England and set in a magnificent deer park The original 15th century house was enlarged in 1603 by the Earl of Dorset and is today the family home of Lord Sackville. Wesley visited on two occasions – in 1780 and ten years later.

Perhaps one of the most important gatherings at which Wesley preached in 1768 was at Chatham (F20) where he addressed a meeting of over two hundred soldiers in the chapel of the local barracks. On another occasion he was given a tour of the dockyard.

Canterbury (F23) was always a favourite place with Wesley for obvious reasons. It is the cradle of English history and religion, dominated by the soaring Bell Harry Tower of its magnificent cathedral. The square half-mile of the medieval city, its walls built on Roman stonework, contains some of the finest examples of ecclesiastical and domestic buildings in Britain. John Wesley preached in the city on a number of occasions and in St Peter's Methodist Church is a table he once used at the former King Street Chapel. St Peter's also retains a private letter written by Wesley to one of his leaders named Matthew.

On his return from Georgia in 1738 John Wesley landed at the port of Deal (F25), as brother Charles had done earlier, and stayed for a few days during which time he preached to a large company in a local inn. A few miles down the coast is Dover (F24) where, in 1756, John climbed the hill to Dover Castle and admired its 'amazingly fine situation'. However, in 1770, then a much older man, he found great difficulty in climbing Shakespeare's Cliff. Inland, Wesley visited Tunbridge Wells (F21) where the Countess of Huntingdon owned a house on Mount Ephraim and where she also built one of her famous chapels (this has since been demolished but a plaque remains by the Kent and Sussex Hospital). John preached on 19 January 1778 at a large Presbyterian meeting house which stands at the top of Little Mount Zion off High Street. It is now used as business premises. At Dorking (E15) in Surrey the earliest chapel opened by Wesley was in 1772 and is identifiable from its iron railings and gateway. It now forms the back of premises of a shop in West Street and is of much architectural interest.

For two hundred years before the Norman Conquest, Winchester in Hampshire was the capital of Wessex. It is one of the great cathedral cities and Wesley took the opportunity to look around in 1771. Eight years later he addressed 4,500 French prisoners and preached on Portsmouth Common that same evening. On a later visit to Winchester he was offered the pulpit of a church by the clergyman but the key went missing. Not to be beaten, he preached in the open air near Westgate and later went along to meet and address two hundred Dutch prisoners.

Rye in East Sussex was once a thriving seaport – one of the

Cinque Ports – and in the Middle Ages the sea came right up to the walls of the hill town which enjoyed a thriving fishing industry. However, with the silting up of its harbour the trade began to die and in the 18th century Rye's economy rested mainly on the proceeds of wool and spirits smuggling. The situation grieved Wesley and he wrote a tract called *A Word to a Smuggler*. He quotes in his Journal 'I find the people willing to hear the good Word at Rye but they will not part with their accursed smuggling'. A similar situation existed at Winchelsea (F22), another of the Cinque Ports, which Wesley first visited in 1771. The townsfolk were so taken with his preaching that they decided to build a preaching house of their own, Winchelsea Chapel. Four years later he returned to the chapel to address his people and was in the town again on 7 October 1790 to preach his last open-air sermon under a tree on the text 'The kingdom of heaven is at hand; repent; and believe the Gospel'. An ash tree, close to the parish church, has since replaced the original and there is a commemorative plaque at its foot. (A year earlier, news had arrived from across the English Channel in France that the Bastille had been stormed and captured by a mob in Paris – the start of the French Revolution – when many of the Royal family and members of the aristocracy were to lose their heads at the guillotine.) One block west of the Winchelsea churchyard is the Methodist chapel, opened in 1785, which retains many original features.

Though still reasonably active, the ageing process began to overtake John Wesley. He preached his very last sermon on 23 February 1791 in the dining room of Kingston House, now demolished, owned by Mr Belson in the centre of Leatherhead, Surrey (E16). A plaque on the local council offices records the fact. Within a few days of this event his earthly life of service to his Lord and Master Jesus Christ would draw to its close.

# CHAPTER 21

# Eventide

THE DAY AFTER preaching his last sermon at Leatherhead, John Wesley, returning to his London home, wrote a letter from Balham in support of William Wilberforce. Wilberforce was a new Member of Parliament who had begun a personal campaign for the abolition of the slave trade. It was very much in tune with Wesley's own feelings on the subject as, years before, he had published a tract of his own entitled *Thoughts upon Slavery*. Along with the daily entry in his Journal this was probably the last thing John ever wrote as his bodily faculties began to fail. (During his lifetime he is attributed to have written over two thousand letters. He was also responsible for writing or editing at least 390 publications including some in Hebrew, Greek, French and English and books on medicine as well as religious works). He lay dying for a few days surrounded by some of his closest friends. Finally, on 2 March 1791, he rallied slightly, prayed, and managed to utter his final words. Shortly afterwards, a few minutes before ten o'clock in the morning, he slipped peacefully away. He was nearly 88 years old.

It was the end of a great life and nobody in 18th century Britain could have been so well known amongst every branch of society. His influence and achievements had been enormous. During the closing years of his life he was no longer persecuted, though persecution of some of his preachers was to continue. In Wesley's place stood the army of Methodist itinerant preachers to take the Word of God to his many societies and anyone who would listen. It is estimated that in over fifty years of evangelising, John Wesley preached at least 40,000 sermons – often speaking several times each day – and travelled around 250,000 miles (400,000 km) – mainly on horseback but in a chaise in later years.

His Journal of missionary travel serves almost as a guide-book to the British Isles. At the time of his death, he left behind a Methodist movement of about 70,000 members.

John's body was visited by a large number of people both in the house and the nearby Wesley's Chapel where it lay awaiting burial. In order to avoid large crowds of people on the day of the funeral on 9 March, the ceremony was held at five in the morning. Those in attendance were each given a commemorative biscuit bearing an effigy of John Wesley. He was interred in a vault prominently marked by an obelisk to the rear of the chapel. (Martha Hall, one of the Wesley sisters, is buried in the same vault along with some of his most notable preachers). John's body was recoffined in 1828. In addition to the inscribed tomb, there is a marble tablet within the chapel and the Adams-Acton statue of Wesley in front of the building. Of other memorials, the most notable are the statue in the north-west corner of St Paul's Cathedral churchyard, and a tablet in Westminster Abbey on the south side of the South Aisle with profile likenesses of John and Charles Wesley. The National Portrait Gallery in St Martin's Lane has John's portrait by Nathaniel Hone (1766), another by William Hamilton (1789), and a marble bust. Other artefacts are kept at the Museum of Methodism at Wesley's Chapel and Wesley's House, City Road, London.

Charles Wesley had died in 1788. He was buried in the graveyard of Old Marylebone Church and the site is now laid out as a sunken garden, the most prominent memorial being an obelisk in memory of Charles and Sarah Wesley and their two sons, all buried there. Access is from Marylebone High Street. His London home was at No.1 Chesterfield Street (now Wheatley Street), situated between Wesley Street and Westmoreland Street, the site now marked by a plaque on the King's Head hostelry. He is probably best remembered as the writer of over seven thousand hymns, many of which are still sung today. Charles eventually found that his work tied him to London, though his family continued to live in Bristol until 1771 when they joined him in the capital. It was then that he began to realise that separation from the Church of England was becoming inevitable – something he was vehemently opposed to.

Under English law, Dissenting preachers and chapels had to be registered to avoid prosecution and, eventually, John Wesley had to agree that Methodists fell into the same category as Congregationalists and Baptists. Hence, he advised that all Methodist preachers and preaching houses should be licensed by law and be known as 'preachers of the Gospel' and 'Methodist chapels'. In 1784 Wesley went a step further by signing a Deed of Declaration, giving legal status to the Conference of Methodist preachers after his death. This constituted the charter of Wesleyan Methodism and the beginning of its modern history. In the same year was the end of the American War of Independence when practically all Anglican clergy fled from rebel states. American Methodists badgered Wesley to try and persuade English bishops to restore some of the clergy in order to allow them to take Holy Communion from an ordained priest. The Anglican church refused and so Wesley sent Dr Thomas Coke to America to ordain Francis Asbury as its first Bishop. The ceremony took place at the

*John Wesley's Tomb*

Baltimore Conference on 24 December 1784. The Methodist Episcopal Church was established in America.

The final piece of the jigsaw was in place in 1795 when the Methodist Church in Britain separated from the Church of England.

Methodism in the 18th century was often looked upon as somewhat revolutionary. It has also been suggested that its growth was one of the reasons why a revolution similar to the French Revolution did not take place in Britain. As with other surges of radicalism, Methodism began to move on into more 'refined' stages – a time when this new group of worshippers wished to settle into a respectable Church of their own. However, there were still factions of extremists who wanted to go further. It was these elements which began to fester after the death of John Wesley.

By 1800, Methodism was splitting into two halves – the more Anglican form, later to be known as Wesleyan Methodism, and the more radical form known as the Methodist New Connexion, founded 1797. Within thirty years of Wesley's death other Methodist churches had appeared – the Primitive Methodists who were formally established in 1812; and the Bible Christians formed in 1815. However, in 1907 a union took place which included the first and the last-named with the United Methodist Free Churches under the name of United Methodist Church. Eventually full union was achieved in 1932 when The Methodist Church was re-constituted. In Britain, the Church is organised into 'circuits', themselves grouped into 33 Districts. The Annual Conference is the governing body of the church.

The quotation by John Wesley – 'The World is my Parish' – became a reality as Methodism spread to almost every country in the world. Its total membership today stands at around seventy million people.

Belatedly, but in order to celebrate the centenary of John Wesley's death, the Methodist Central Hall in Westminster was opened in 1912. It stands in a prime location opposite Westminster Abbey overlooking Parliament Square and the

Palace of Westminster, the seat of Government. The design was chosen from over one hundred entries in an architectural competition. The building has a huge dome and contains Viennese Baroque architecture with Romanesque decoration. The Great Hall is used for many events, both national and international, as well as church services, and contains a huge pipe organ with 4,731 pipes. The inaugural meeting of the United Nations General Assembly was held in Westminster Central Hall in 1946. At the top of the Grand Staircase stands a statue of John Wesley by sculptor Samuel Manning, commissioned in 1830.

As we gaze at this statue of John Wesley with a Bible in one hand and the other slightly raised, we can reflect on his momentous life and influence and also maybe recall the famous words he uttered on his deathbed – 'THE BEST OF ALL IS, GOD IS WITH US!'

# Useful addresses

## *Britain*

British Tourist Authority
Thames Tower
Black's Road
Hammersmith
London W6 9EL
Tel: 020 8846 9000

Churches Conservation Trust
89 Fleet Street
London EC4Y 1DH
Tel: 020 7936 2285

English Tourism Council
Thames Tower
Black's Road
Hammersmith
London W6 9EL
Tel: 020 8563 3354

Methodist Church House
25 Marylebone Road
London NW1 5JR
Tel: 020 7486 5502

Wesley's Chapel, House and Museum of Methodism
49 City Road
London EC1Y 1AU
Tel: 020 7253 2262

Methodist Central Hall
Storey's Gate
Westminster
London SW1H 9NH
Tel: 020 7222 8010

St Paul's Cathedral
The Chapter House
St Paul's Churchyard
London EC4M 8AD
Tel: 020 7236 4128

Moravian Centre
381 Kings Road, Chelsea
London SW10 0LP
Tel: 020 7352 2624

Wesley Centre
Kingswood School
Lansdown Road
Bath, Somerset BA1 5RG
Tel: 01225 734352

Coleg Trefeca
Nr. Talgarth
Brecon, Powys LD3 0PP
Tel: 01874 711423

John Wesley's Chapel (The 'New Room')
36 The Horsefair
Bristol BS1 3JE
Tel: 0117 926 4740

Wesley College
College Park Drive
Henbury Road
Bristol BS10 7QD
Tel: 0117 959 1200

The Old Rectory
1 Rectory Street
Epworth
Nr. Doncaster
South Yorkshire DN9 1HX
Tel: 01427 872268

John Rylands University Library (Methodist Archives)
150 Deansgate
Manchester M3 3EH
Tel: 0161 834 5343

Museum of Primitive Methodism
Engelsea Brook
Crewe
Cheshire CW2 5QD
Tel: 01270 820836 or 01782 810109

Christ Church – College and Cathedral
St Aldates
Oxford OX1 1DP
Tel: 01865 286573 (general enquiries)
Tel: 01865 276492 (tours – Head Custodian)

Lincoln College
Turl Street
Oxford OX1 3DR
Tel: 01865 279815

Wesley and Methodist Studies Centre
Westminster Institute of Education
Oxford Brookes University
Oxford OX2 9AT
Tel: 01865 488286

British Methodist Heritage on the internet: for
more specific details of many heritage sites
www.forsaith-oxon.demon.co.uk/methodist-heritage

# USA

British Tourist Authority
625 North Michigan Avenue
Suite 1001
Chicago, Illinois 60611
(Personal callers only, Mon – Fri)

British Tourist Authority
7th Floor, 551 Fifth Avenue
New York NY 10176-0799
Tel: 00 1(212) 986 2266
www.travelbritain.org

South Georgia Conference of the
United Methodist Church (US)
Epworth by the Sea
Box 20407
St Simon's Island
Georgia 31522
Tel: 00 1 (912) 638 4050

Georgia Dept. of Industry, Trade & Tourism
285 Peachtree Center
Avenue, NE Marquis Two Tower
Suite 1100
Atlanta
Georgia 30303-1230
Tel: 00 1 (404) 463 3914

Savannah Visitors Center
301 Martin Luther King Jr. Blvd
Savannah
Georgia 31401
Tel: 00 1 (912) 944-0455

# Bibliography

Beckerlegge, Oliver A — *John Wesley comes to York,* Quacks Printers, York, 1988.

Capon, John — *John & Charles Wesley: The Preacher and The Poet,* Hodder & Stoughton, London, 1988.

Cheetham, J Keith — *On the Trail of the Pilgrim Fathers,* Luath Press Ltd, Edinburgh, 2001.

Dedman, Stanley C — *Westbrook and the Oglethorpes,* Trustees of Godalming Museum, 1990.

Davey, Cyril — *John Wesley and the Methodists,* Marshall Morgan & Scott Ltd, 1985.

Edwards, Dr Maldwyn — *My Dear Sister,* Penwork (Leeds) Ltd, Manchester.

Gill, Frederick C — *In the Steps of John Wesley,* Lutterworth Press, London, 1962.

Haire, Robert — *Wesley's One-and-Twenty Visits to Ireland,* The Epworth Press 1947.

Harmon, Rebecca Lamar — *Susanna, Mother of the Wesleys,* Hodder & Stoughton Ltd, London, 1968.

Heatherington, David — *John Wesley's Journeys Through Weardale,* Weardale Museum, 1993.

Joselin, Eric S — *John Wesley – Incomparable Itinerant*, Rev ES Joselin, 2002.

Leach, Terence R — *John Wesley's Earthly Paradise*, Lace Books, Dunholme, Lincoln, 1993.

Lean, Garth — *John Wesley, Anglican*, Blandford Press Ltd, London, 1964.

Monk, Robert C — *John Wesley – His Puritan Heritage*, Epworth Press, London, 1966.

Pratt, Alfred C — *Black Country Methodism*, Charles H Kelly, London, 1891.

Rack, Henry D — *Reasonable Enthusiast*, Epworth Press, London, 1989.

Thorold, Henry — *Lincolnshire*, Faber & Faber, London, 1965.

Vickers, Dr John A — *John Wesley – Founder of Methodism*, Methodist Publishing House, Peterborough.

# Some other books published by **LUATH** PRESS

## On the Trail of the Pilgrim Fathers
J. Keith Cheetham
ISBN 0 946487 83 9  PBK £7.99

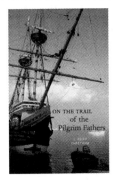

The fascinating, true story of the founding fathers of the United States, their origins in England and their harrowing journey to a New World.

After harvest time in 1621 around 60 men, women and children held a great feast in gratitude to God to celebrate their deliverance and the first anniversary of their leaving England to found a settlement in North America. These people became known as the Pilgrim Fathers. The feast was repeated annually and became known as Thanksgiving. Almost 400 years later, US citizens still celebrate Thanksgiving. But who were the Pilgrim Fathers?

The political situation in 16th and 17th century England was such that those who differed from the established church were persecuted, punished and humiliated. The Puritans determined to leave English shores rather than submit to changing their beliefs.

In this account, Keith Cheetham tells of their flight to Holland, their subsequent departure from Plymouth on the Mayflower in September 1620 and the perils that faced them in the New World. These are true stories of tragedy and danger as well as success.

Over 170 places to visit in England, Holland and the USA

One general map, 4 location maps of England, 1 of Holland and 1 of New England

Line drawings and illustrations

List of names of those who sailed in the Mayflower.

As in his earlier book, On the Trail of Mary Queen of Scots, Keith Cheetham once again gives a thorough guide to the origins and places connected with these early settlers. He sets their achievements in the context of earlier European explorers to the New World.

On the Trail of the Pilgrim Fathers is for everyone interested in the brave folk who left the Old World for the New.

'They will conform or I will harry them out of the land'
KING JAMES I OF ENGLAND

'As one small candle may light a thousand, so the light here kindled hath shone to many'
WILLIAM BRADFORD, GOVERNOR, PLYMOUTH PLANTATION

## On the Trail of Mary Queen of Scots

J. Keith Cheetham

ISBN 0 946487 50 2 PBK £7.99

Life dealt Mary Queen of Scots love, intrigue, betrayal and tragedy in generous measure.

*On the Trail of Mary Queen of Scots* traces the major events in the turbulent life of the beautiful, enigmatic queen whose romantic reign and tragic destiny exerts an undimmed fascination over 400 years after her execution.

Places of interest to visit – 99 in Scotland, 35 in England and 29 in France.

One general map and 6 location maps.

Line drawings and illustrations.

Simplified family tree of the royal houses of Tudor and Stuart.

Key sites include:

Linlithgow Palace – Mary's birthplace, now a magnificent ruin

Stirling Castle – where, only nine months old, Mary was crowned Queen of Scotland

Notre Dame Cathedral – where, aged fifteen, she married the future king of France

The Palace of Holyroodhouse – Rizzio, one of Mary's closest advisers, was murdered here and some say his blood still stains the spot where he was stabbed to death

Sheffield Castle – where for fourteen years she languished as prisoner of her cousin, Queen Elizabeth I

Fotheringhay – here Mary finally met her death on the executioner's block.

*On the Trail of Mary Queen of Scots* is for everyone interested in the life of perhaps the most romantic figure in Scotland's history; a thorough guide to places connected with Mary, it is also a guide to the complexities of her personal and public life.

*'In my end is my beginning'*
MARY QUEEN OF SCOTS

*'...the woman behaves like the Whore of Babylon'* JOHN KNOX

## On the Trail of William Wallace

David R. Ross

ISBN 0 946487 47 2 PBK £7.99

How close to reality was *Braveheart*?

Where was Wallace actually born?

What was the relationship between Wallace and Bruce?

Are there any surviving eye-witness accounts of Wallace?

How does Wallace influence the psyche of today's Scots?

*On the Trail of William Wallace* offers a refreshing insight into the life and heritage of the great Scots hero whose proud story is at the very heart of what it means to be Scottish. Not concentrating simply on the hard historical facts of Wallace's life, the book also takes into account the real significance of Wallace and his effect on the ordinary Scot through the ages, manifested in the many sites where his memory is marked.

In trying to piece together the jigsaw of the reality of Wallace's life, David Ross weaves a subtle flow of new information with his own observations. His engaging, thoughtful and at times amusing narrative reads with the ease of a historical novel, complete with all the intrigue, treachery and romance required to hold the attention of the casual reader and still entice the more knowledgable historian.

74 places to visit in Scotland and the north of England

One general map and 3 location maps

Stirling and Falkirk battle plans

Wallace's route through London

Chapter on Wallace connections in North America and elsewhere

Reproductions of rarely seen illustrations

*On the Trail of William Wallace* will be enjoyed by anyone with an interest in Scotland, from the passing tourist to the most fervent nationalist. It is an encyclopaedia-cum-guide book, literally stuffed with fascinating titbits not usually on offer in the conventional history book.

David Ross is organiser of and historical adviser to the Society of William Wallace.

*'Historians seem to think all there is to be known about Wallace has already been uncovered. Mr Ross has proved that Wallace studies are in fact in their infancy.'*
ELSPETH KING, Director the the Stirling Smith Art Museum & Gallery, who annotated and introduced the recent Luath edition of *Blind Harry's Wallace*.

*'Better the pen than the sword!'*
RANDALL WALLACE, author of *Braveheart*, when asked by David Ross how it felt to be partly responsible for the freedom of a nation following the Devolution Referendum.

## On the Trail of Robert the Bruce

David R. Ross

ISBN 0 946487 52 9  PBK  £7.99

*On the Trail of Robert the Bruce* charts the story of Scotland's hero-king from his boyhood, through his days of indecision as Scotland suffered under the English yoke, to his assumption of the crown exactly six months after the death of William Wallace. Here is the astonishing blow by blow account of how, against fearful odds, Bruce led the Scots to win their greatest ever victory. Bannockburn was not the end of the story. The war against English oppression lasted another fourteen years. Bruce lived just long enough to see his dreams of an independent Scotland come to fruition in 1328 with the signing of the Treaty of Edinburgh. The trail takes us to Bruce sites in Scotland, many of the little known and forgotten battle sites in northern England, and as far afield as the Bruce monuments in Andalusia and Jerusalem.

67 places to visit in Scotland and elsewhere.

One general map, 3 location maps and a map of Bruce-connected sites in Ireland.

Bannockburn battle plan.

Drawings and reproductions of rarely seen illustrations.

*On the Trail of Robert the Bruce* is not all blood and gore. It brings out the love and laughter, pain and passion of one of the great eras of Scottish history. Read it and you will understand why David Ross has never knowingly killed a spider in his life. Once again, he proves himself a master of the popular brand of hands-on history that made *On the Trail of William Wallace* so popular.

*'David R. Ross is a proud patriot and unashamed romantic.'*
SCOTLAND ON SUNDAY

*'Robert the Bruce knew Scotland, knew every class of her people, as no man who ruled her before or since has done. It was he who asked of her a miracle - and she accomplished it.'*
AGNES MUIR MACKENZIE

## On the Trail of Robert Service

GW Lockhart

ISBN 0 946487 24 3 PBK £7.99

Robert Service is famed world-wide for his eye-witness verse-pictures of the Klondike goldrush. As a war poet, his work outsold Owen and Sassoon, and he went on to become the world's first million selling poet. In search of adventure and new experiences, he emigrated from Scotland to Canada in 1890 where he was caught up in the aftermath of the raging gold fever. His vivid dramatic verse bring to life the wild, larger than life characters of the gold rush Yukon, their bar-room brawls, their lust for gold, their trigger-happy gambles with life and love. 'The Shooting of Dan McGrew' is perhaps his most famous poem:

> A bunch of the boys were whooping it up
> in the Malamute saloon;
> The kid that handles the music box was
> hitting a ragtime tune;
> Back of the bar in a solo game, sat
> Dangerous Dan McGrew,
> And watching his luck was his light
> o'love, the lady that's known as Lou.

His storytelling powers have brought Robert Service enduring fame, particularly in North America and Scotland where he is something of a cult figure. Starting in Scotland, *On the Trail of Robert Service* follows Service as he wanders through British Columbia, Oregon, California, Mexico, Cuba, Tahiti, Russia, Turkey and the Balkans, finally 'settling' in France.

This revised edition includes an expanded selection of illustrations of scenes from the Klondike as well as several photographs from the family of Robert Service on his travels around the world. Wallace Lockhart, an expert on Scottish traditional folk music and dance, is the author of *Highland Balls & Village Halls* and *Fiddles & Folk*. His relish for a well-told tale in popular vernacular led him to fall in love with the verse of Robert Service and write his biography.

'*A fitting tribute to a remarkable man - a bank clerk who wanted to become a cowboy. It is hard to imagine a bank clerk writing such lines as:*
> *A bunch of boys were whooping it up...*
*The income from his writing actually exceeded his bank salary by a factor of five and he resigned to pursue a full time writing career.*' Charles Munn,
THE SCOTTISH BANKER

'*Robert Service claimed he wrote for those who wouldnit be seen dead reading poetry. His was an almost unbelievably mobile life... Lockhart hangs on breathlessly, enthusiastically unearthing clues to the poet's life.*'
Ruth Thomas,
SCOTTISH BOOK COLLECTOR

'*This enthralling biography will delight Service lovers in both the Old World and the New.*' Marilyn Wright,
SCOTS INDEPENDENT

## On the Trail of John Muir

Cherry Good

ISBN 0 946487 62 6 PBK £7.99

Follow the man who made the US go green. Confidant of presidents, father of American National Parks, trailblazer of world conservation and voted a Man of the Millennium in the US, John Muir's life and work is of continuing relevance. A man ahead of his time who saw the wilderness he loved threatened by industrialisation and determined to protect it, a crusade in which he was largely successful. His love of the wilderness began at an early age and he was filled with wanderlust all his life.

*Only by going in silence, without baggage, can on truly get into the heart of the wilderness. All other travel is mere dust and hotels and baggage and chatter.* JOHN MUIR

Braving mosquitoes and black bears Cherry Good set herself on his trail – Dunbar, Scotland; Fountain Lake and Hickory Hill, Wisconsin; Yosemite Valley and the Sierra Nevada, California; the Grand Canyon, Arizona; Alaska; and Canada – to tell his story. John Muir was himself a prolific writer, and Good draws on his books, articles, letters and diaries to produce an account that is lively, intimate, humorous and anecdotal, and that provides refreshing new insights into the hero of world conservation.

John Muir chronology

General map plus 10 detailed maps covering the US, Canada and Scotland

Original colour photographs

Afterword advises on how to get involved

Conservation websites and addresses

Muir's importance has long been acknowledged in the US with over 200 sites of scenic beauty named after him. He was a Founder of The Sierra Club which now has over ¹/₂ million members. Due to the movement he started some 360 million acres of wilderness are now protected. This is a book which shows Muir not simply as a hero but as likeable humorous and self-effacing man of extraordinary vision.

*'I do hope that those who read this book will burn with the same enthusiasm for John Muir which the author shows.'*
WEST HIGHLAND FREE PRESS

## On the Trail of Robert Burns

John Cairney
ISBN 0 946487 51 0  PBK  £7.99
Is there anything new to say about Robert Burns?

John Cairney says it's time to trash Burns

the Brand and come on the trail of the real Robert Burns. He is the best of travelling companions on this convivial, entertaining journey to the heart of the Burns story.

Internationally known as 'the face of Robert Burns', John Cairney believes that the traditional Burns tourist trail urgently needs to find a new direction. In an acting career spanning forty years he has often lived and breathed Robert Burns on stage. *On the Trail of Robert Burns* shows just how well he can get under the skin of a character. This fascinating journey around Scotland is a rediscovery of Scotland's national bard as a flesh and blood genius.

*On the Trail of Robert Burns* outlines five tours, mainly in Scotland. Key sites include:

Alloway - Burns' birthplace. 'Tam O' Shanter' draws on the witch-stories about Alloway Kirk first heard by Burns in his childhood.
Mossgiel - between 1784 and 1786 in a phenomenal burst of creativity Burns wrote some of his most memorable poems including 'Holy Willie's Prayer' and 'To a Mouse.'
Kilmarnock - the famous Kilmarnock edition of *Poems Chiefly in the Scottish Dialect*
published in 1786.
Edinburgh - fame and Clarinda (among others) embraced him.
Dumfries - Burns died at the age of 37. The trail ends at the Burns mausoleum in St Michael's churchyard.

*'For me an aim I never fash*
*I rhyme for fun'* ROBERT BURNS

*'My love affair on stage with Burns started in London in 1959. It was consumated on stage at the Traverse Theatre in Edinburgh in 1965 and has continued happily ever since'*
JOHN CAIRNEY

## ON THE TRAIL OF

**On the Trail of Bonnie Prince Charlie**
David R Ross
ISBN 0 946487 68 5  PB  £7.99

**On the Trail of Robert Burns**
John Cairney
ISBN 0 946487 51 0  PB  £7.99

**On the Trail of Queen Victoria in the Highlands**
Ian R Mitchell
ISBN 0 946487 79 0  PB  £7.99

## THE QUEST FOR

**The Quest for the Celtic Key**
Karen Ralls-MacLeod and
Ian Robertson
ISBN 0 946487 73 1  HB  £18.99

**The Quest for Arthur**
Stuart McHardy
ISBN 1 842820 12 5  HB  £16.99

**The Quest for the Nine Maidens**
Stuart McHardy
ISBN 0 946487 66 9  HB  £16.99

## POLITICS & CURRENT ISSUES

**Scotlands of the Mind**
Angus Calder
ISBN 1 84282 008 7  PB  £9.99

**Trident on Trial: the case for people's disarmament**
Angie Zelter
ISBN 1 84282 004 4  PB  £9.99

**Uncomfortably Numb: A Prison Requiem**
Maureen Maguire
ISBN 1 84282 001 X  PB  £8.99

**Scotland: Land & Power – Agenda for Land Reform**
Andy Wightman
ISBN 0 946487 70 7  PB  £5.00

**Old Scotland New Scotland**
Jeff Fallow
ISBN 0 946487 40 5  PB  £6.99

**Some Assembly Required: Scottish Parliament**
David Shepherd
ISBN 0 946487  84 7  PB  £7.99

**Notes from the North**
Emma Wood
ISBN 0 946487 46 4  PB  £8.99

## NATURAL WORLD

**The Hydro Boys: pioneers of renewable energy**
Emma Wood
ISBN 1 84282 016 8  HB  £16.99

**Wild Scotland**
James McCarthy
ISBN 0 946487 37 5  PB  £7.50

**Wild Lives: Otters – On the Swirl of the Tide**
Bridget MacCaskill
ISBN 0 946487 67 7  PB  £9.99

**Wild Lives: Foxes – The Blood is Wild**
Bridget MacCaskill
ISBN 0 946487 71 5  PB  £9.99

**Scotland – Land & People: An Inhabited Solitude**
James McCarthy
ISBN 0 946487 57 X  PB  £7.99

**The Highland Geology Trail**
John L Roberts
ISBN 0 946487 36 7  PB  £4.99

**'Nothing but Heather!'**
Gerry Cambridge
ISBN 0 946487 49 9  PB  £15.00

**Red Sky at Night**
John Barrington
ISBN 0 946487 60 X  PB  £8.99

**Listen to the Trees**
Don MacCaskill
ISBN 0 946487 65 0  PB  £9.99

## ISLANDS

**The Islands that Roofed the World: Easdale, Belnahua, Luing & Seil:**
Mary Withall
ISBN 0 946487 76 6  PB  £4.99

**Rum: Nature's Island**
Magnus Magnusson
ISBN 0 946487 32 4  PB  £7.95

## LUATH GUIDES TO SCOTLAND

**The North West Highlands: Roads to the Isles**
Tom Atkinson
ISBN 0 946487 54 5  PB  £4.95

**Mull and Iona: Highways and Byways**
Peter Macnab
ISBN 0 946487 58 8  PB  £4.95

**The Northern Highlands: The Empty Lands**
Tom Atkinson
ISBN 0 946487 55 3   PB  £4.95

**The West Highlands: The Lonely Lands**
Tom Atkinson
ISBN 0 946487 56 1  PB  £4.95

**South West Scotland**
Tom Atkinson
ISBN 0 946487 04 9  PB  £4.95

## TRAVEL & LEISURE

**Die Kleine Schottlandfibel [Scotland Guide in German]**
Hans-Walter Arends
ISBN 0 946487 89 8  PB  £8.99

**Let's Explore Edinburgh Old Town**
Anne Bruce English
ISBN 0 946487 98 7  PB  £4.99

**Edinburgh's Historic Mile**
Duncan Priddle
ISBN 0 946487 97 9  PB  £2.99

**Pilgrims in the Rough: St Andrews beyond the 19th hole**
Michael Tobert
ISBN 0 946487 74 X  PB  £7.99

## FOOD & DRINK

**The Whisky Muse: Scotch whisky in poem & song**
various, ed. Robin Laing
ISBN 0 946487 95 2  PB  £12.99

**First Foods Fast: good simple baby meals**
Lara Boyd
ISBN 1 84282 002 8  PB  £4.99

**Edinburgh and Leith Pub Guide**
Stuart McHardy
ISBN 0 946487 80 4  PB  £4.95

## WALK WITH LUATH

**Skye 360: walking the coastline of Skye**
Andrew Dempster
ISBN 0 946487 85 5  PB  £8.99

**Walks in the Cairngorms**
Ernest Cross
ISBN 0 946487 09 X  PB  £4.95

**Short Walks in the Cairngorms**
Ernest Cross
ISBN 0 946487 23 5  PB  £4.95

**The Joy of Hillwalking**
Ralph Storer
ISBN 0 946487 28 6  PB  £7.50

**Scotland's Mountains before the Mountaineers**
Ian R Mitchell
ISBN 0 946487 39 1  PB  £9.99

**Mountain Days and Bothy Nights**
Dave Brown and Ian R Mitchell
ISBN 0 946487 15 4  PB  £7.50

## SPORT

**Ski & Snowboard Scotland**
Hilary Parke
ISBN 0 946487 35 9  PB  £6.99

**Over the Top with the Tartan Army**
Andy McArthur
ISBN 0 946487 45 6  PB  £7.99

## BIOGRAPHY

**The Last Lighthouse**
Sharma Krauskopf
ISBN 0 946487 96 0  PB  £7.99

**Tobermory Teuchter**
Peter Macnab
ISBN 0 946487 41 3  PB  £7.99

**Bare Feet and Tackety Boots**
Archie Cameron
ISBN 0 946487 17 0  PB  £7.95

**Come Dungeons Dark**
John Taylor Caldwell
ISBN 0 946487 19 7  PB  £6.95

## HISTORY

**Civil Warrior**
Robin Bell
ISBN 1 84282 013 3  HB  £10.99

**A Passion for Scotland**
David R Ross
ISBN 1 84282 019 2  PB  £5.99

**Reportage Scotland**
Louise Yeoman
ISBN 0 946487 61 8  PB  £9.99

**Blind Harry's Wallace**
Hamilton of Gilbertfield
introduced by Elspeth King
ISBN 0 946487 33 2  PB  £8.99

## SOCIAL HISTORY

**Pumpherston: the story of a shale oil village**
Sybil Cavanagh
ISBN 1 84282 011 7  HB  £17.99

**Pumpherston: the story of a shale oil village**
Sybil Cavanagh
ISBN 1 84282 015 X  PB  £7.99

**Shale Voices**
Alistair Findlay
ISBN 0 946487 78 2  HB  £17.99

**Shale Voices**
Alistair Findlay
ISBN 0 946487 63 4  PB  £10.99

**A Word for Scotland**
Jack Campbell
ISBN 0 946487 48 0  PB  £12.99

## FOLKLORE

**Scotland: Myth, Legend & Folklore**
Stuart McHardy
ISBN 0 946487 69 3  PB  £7.99

**Luath Storyteller: Highland Myths & Legends**
George W Macpherson
ISBN 1 84282 003 6  PB  £5.00

**Tales of the North Coast**
Alan Temperley
ISBN 0 946487 18 9  PB  £8.99

**Tall Tales from an Island**
Peter Macnab
ISBN 0 946487 07 3  PB  £8.99

**The Supernatural Highlands**
Francis Thompson
ISBN 0 946487 31 6  PB  £8.99

## GENEALOGY

**Scottish Roots: step-by-step guide for ancestor hunters**
Alwyn James
ISBN 1 84282 007 9  PB  £9.99

## WEDDINGS, MUSIC AND DANCE

**The Scottish Wedding Book**
G Wallace Lockhart
ISBN 1 94282 010 9  PB  £12.99

**Fiddles and Folk**
G Wallace Lockhart
ISBN 0 946487 38 3  PB  £7.95

**Highland Balls and Village Halls**
G Wallace Lockhart
ISBN 0 946487 12 X  PB  £6.95

## POETRY

**Bad Ass Raindrop**
Kokumo Rocks
ISBN 1 84282 018 4  PB  £6.99

**Caledonian Cramboclink: the Poetry of**
William Neill
ISBN 0 946487 53 7  PB  £8.99

**Men and Beasts: wild men & tame animals**
Val Gillies & Rebecca Marr
ISBN 0 946487 92 8  PB  £15.00

**Luath Burns Companion**
John Cairney
ISBN 1 84282 000 1  PB  £10.00

**Scots Poems to be read aloud**
intro Stuart McHardy
ISBN 0 946487 81 2  PB  £5.00

**Poems to be read aloud**
various
ISBN 0 946487 00 6  PB  £5.00

**Picking Brambles and Other Poems**
Des Dillon
ISBN 1 84282 021 4  PB  £6.99

**Kate o Shanter's Tale and Other Poems**
Matthew Fitt
ISBN 1 84282 028 1  PB  £6.99

## CARTOONS

**Broomie Law**
Cinders McLeod
ISBN 0 946487 99 5  PB  £4.00

## FICTION

**The Road Dance**
John MacKay
ISBN 1 84282 024 9  PB  £9.99

**Milk Treading**
Nick Smith
ISBN 0 946487 75 8  PB  £9.99

**The Strange Case of RL Stevenson**
Richard Woodhead
ISBN 0 946487 86 3  HB  £16.99

**But n Ben A-Go-Go**
Matthew Fitt
ISBN 1 84282 014 1  PB  £6.99

**But n Ben A-Go-Go**
Matthew Fitt
ISBN 0 946487 82 0  HB  £10.99

**Grave Robbers**
Robin Mitchell
ISBN 0 946487 72 3  PB  £7.99

**The Bannockburn Years**
William Scott
ISBN 0 946487 34 0  PB  £7.95

**The Great Melnikov**
Hugh MacLachlan
ISBN 0 946487 42 1  PB  £7.95

**The Fundamentals of New Caledonia**
David Nicol
ISBN 0 946487 93 6  HB  £16.99

## LANGUAGE

**Luath Scots Language Learner [Book]**
L Colin Wilson
ISBN 0 946487 91 X  PB  £9.99

**Luath Scots Language Learner [Double Audio CD Set]**
L Colin Wilson
ISBN 1 84282 026 5  CD  £16.99

## **Luath** Press Limited

*committed to publishing well written books worth reading*

LUATH PRESS takes its name from Robert Burns, whose little collie Luath (*Gael.*, swift or nimble) tripped up Jean Armour at a wedding and gave him the chance to speak to the woman who was to be his wife and the abiding love of his life. Burns called one of *The Twa Dogs* Luath after Cuchullin's hunting dog in *Ossian's Fingal*. Luath Press grew up in the heart of Burns country, and now resides a few steps up the road from Burns' first lodgings in Edinburgh's Royal Mile.

Luath offers you distinctive writing with a hint of unexpected pleasures.

Most UK bookshops either carry our books in stock or can order them for you. To order direct from us, please send a £sterling cheque, postal order, international money order or your credit card details (number, address of cardholder and expiry date) to us at the address below. Please add post and packing as follows: UK – £1.00 per delivery address; overseas surface mail – £2.50 per delivery address; overseas airmail – £3.50 for the first book to each delivery address, plus £1.00 for each additional book by airmail to the same address. If your order is a gift, we will happily enclose your card or message at no extra charge.

**Luath** Press Limited
543/2 Castlehill
The Royal Mile
Edinburgh EH1 2ND
Scotland

Telephone: 0131 225 4326 (24 hours)
Fax: 0131 225 4324
email: gavin.macdougall@luath.co.uk
Website: www.luath.co.uk